Health:
the strength to be human

HEALTH:
THE STRENGTH
TO BE HUMAN

Edited by Andrew Fergusson

CMF/IVP

INTER-VARSITY PRESS
38 De Montfort Street, Leicester LE1 7PG, England

First published 1993

British Library Cataloguing in Publication Data
A catalogue record for this book is available from the British
Library.

ISBN 0–85110–981–0

Set in Linotron Baskerville
Photoset by Parker Typesetting Service, Leicester
Printed and bound in Great Britain by
Cox & Wyman Ltd, Reading, Berkshire

CONTENTS

ACKNOWLEDGMENTS

The following material is copyright and used by permission:

Extracts from the writings of Donald MacKay which appear on pages 69, 71–72, 75–76, 76–77 and 79–80 are taken from *The Open Mind and Other Essays,* edited by Melvin Tinker (IVP, 1986);

Extracts from J. Neville Ward which appear on pages 93, 94, 95 and 96 are taken from his *The Use of Praying* (Epworth, 1967);

The Appendix to Chapter 7 is reproduced from the *European Charter on Environment and Health* (World Health Organization, 1989);

Extracts appearing on pages 195–196 and 197–198 are taken from *Our Lord's, the Poor* (CMF, 1984);

The extract appearing on page 193 is taken from *Crisis Unawares* (OMF, 1981);

The extract appearing on pages 210–219 is reproduced from *New Directions and Opportunities for Christian Health Care Ministries* (MAP International, 1982).

PREFACE

As the 1980s drew to a close there was considerable debate in Britain about the future of the National Health Service. Many other countries worldwide were having similar discussions. If we are to strive for good health, one fairly obvious question (to which the answer is less obvious) is: What is good health?

To try to answer this question from a Christian perspective, a group of about thirty healthcare workers and theologians met over a weekend in June 1989. At an early point, one definition seemed to attract most of us. The theologian Jürgen Moltmann has rephrased an earlier definition by Karl Barth, saying that health is 'the strength to be human'. Critics have called this definition 'deceptively simple', and of course it is, but its great merits are that it is a definition without theological jargon, one which should engage any reasonable colleague, and above all one which leads to the obvious question: What do we mean by human? This question has some convincing Christian answers.

There were two further tangible outcomes from the weekend. The first was the consensus statement on the nature of health that follows this Preface, which amplified this definition and was given considerable publicity at the time.

The second is this book. Seven of the eight authors were present at the weekend. I am grateful to all eight, but particularly to Peter Pattisson who, without the benefit of participating in the stimulating discussion, nevertheless wrote the vital chapter on worldwide perspectives which concludes the book.

Each author attempts to apply the relevant concepts in the statement to his or her particular area of interest. The result is a wide-ranging Christian view of health in its broadest context, which the whole world needs as we grapple with the seemingly overwhelming problems of the 1990s.

David Atkinson begins with the Bible. His chapter on a theology of health works towards the definition this book is all about. Alan Storkey's chapter is vital to set an understanding of the practice of healthcare in the context of the social, economic and political factors which are bound to shape it. Although largely discussing the British National Health Service, there are important concepts here which are valid worldwide.

Healthcare personnel will immediately feel more at ease with the next three chapters, which relate to individual patients in hospital and primary care from the perspectives of two doctors and a nurse. There is considerable emphasis on spiritual principles which have universal application.

Those working with individual patients always have to remember populations, and so the book turns to a chapter on public health which has some fascinating historical insights. Even examining whole populations is inadequate if no account is taken of the broader context of the environment, and Professor Berry's chapter here is particularly stimulating. The book closes by reminding us how well-off we are in the West, and that God's Word must be expressed in his work in the whole of his world.

I would like to conclude by expressing further gratitude to Ernest Lucas and his colleagues at Christian Impact who did so much to get the discussion rolling, to the members and office staff of Christian Medical Fellowship who facilitated this book, and to Colin Duriez at IVP for patient encouragement.

Andrew Fergusson
General Secretary,
Christian Medical Fellowship.

HEALTH: THE STRENGTH TO BE HUMAN

In order to guide the current debate on health service management and allocation of resources, a group of about thirty Christian healthcare workers and theologians met to discuss the question: Good health – what is it? We favoured the definition of some previous writers:

Health: the strength to be human

Those of other faiths and ideologies should also support this definition, but of course it raises the question: What do we mean by human?

As Christians, we would define human-ness (and hence health) in terms of the following *relationships*:

1. *With God.* We are made in the image of God to have a harmonious relationship with him. Sin destroys this. The harmony is restored through repentance from sin, personal faith in Christ's death on the cross, and acceptance of his lordship in our lives. This makes us spiritually whole.
2. *With self.* Physical disease can occur when different parts of the body fail to inter-relate properly, and psychological disease includes failure to relate healthily to oneself.
3. *With others.* Healthy relationships are needed between individuals, in families, in communities, and in societies, both nationally and internationally.
4. *With the environment.* We should respect God's creation

9

for its own sake and for the benefit of our health.

We must beware the idolatry of 'healthism', where the primary relationship with God is neglected, and there can be an unhealthy obsession with our own state.

Health is linked with wholeness, and is part of the biblical concept of *shalom*. Often translated 'peace', shalom means more than the absence of conflict and involves wholeness, well-being, vigour, and vitality in all the dimensions of human life. This all-embracing definition is an *ideal* one. We may legitimately need to use more specific *functional* definitions of health for particular tasks, but must beware too narrow a view of health.

This broad definition of health leads to the following *applications*:

Public policy on health must mean more than the provision of medical services, and must refer to all the relationships outlined above. For example, spiritual well-being, stable families, better housing, less hazardous workplaces, and safer transport would all improve health, and would in the longer term be cost-effective. Increased taxation on alcohol and tobacco could generate money for healthcare, and by depressing consumption could give more people more strength to be more human.

Resource allocation. We believe there are three important principles which are related and which need to be kept in balance:

1. *Justice*. We should treat people rightly according to need.
2. *Equity*. We should provide equal access to healthcare, according to need, with financial factors being no deterrent.
3. *Concern for the disadvantaged*. We have a responsibility to take particular care of the defenceless. This may require positive discrimination.

Global view. We would emphasize our worldwide responsibility to fellow humans and believe the West should increase genuine aid to healthcare services in developing countries.

Decision-making. We agree that healthcare should always be provided as efficiently as possible, but to judge efficiency by financial measures alone is inappropriate, inadequate, and immoral. We believe the whole community, and not just healthcare professionals, should be involved in making judgments about the allocation of resources.

Christian responsibility. We would encourage the Christian church everywhere to recognize its responsibility to promote healthcare in the broadest sense, and to mobilize its undoubted resources.

July 1989

This consensus statement on the nature of health was produced by members of Caring Professions Concern, Christian Medical Fellowship, The Churches' Council for Health and Healing, Christian Impact, and Nurses' Christian Fellowship.

Part One

Chapter One

TOWARDS A THEOLOGY OF HEALTH

David Atkinson

Fellow and Chaplain, Corpus Christi College, Oxford

Within and outside the Christian church, there is considerable variation in the understanding of concepts of disease, illness and sickness on the one hand, and of health and healing on the other.

Some writers distinguish 'disease', taken to be an objective pathological condition, from 'illness' (which describes a person's subjective perception of disorder within themselves) and from 'sickness' (which is defined socially in terms of a deviation from what society accepts as normal). These distinctions lead to different understandings of healing. Some writers view healing in terms of a medical model of disease, and others in terms of psychological perceptions of illness, or of social definitions of sickness.

More fundamental, however, than these concepts of healing is the concept of health. Healing, however defined, is, at its most basic, movement towards health. But what is health? At a time when the National Health Service in Britain is undergoing its most radical review and reformation since its inception more than forty years ago, it is vital that priorities are re-evaluated and the purpose of the Health Service clarified. We cannot approach such issues without some answer to the question 'What is health?'

This chapter attempts to offer a biblical theological perspective on this question. Before we enter that discussion, however, some further preliminary issues need to be clarified.

Definitions of health

The question 'What is health?' lends itself to almost as many answers as there are questioners. It is hard to achieve a wide consensus on the definition of 'health', and answers range from what we may call a 'minimal' definition, through a whole range of intermediate views, to a 'maximal' definition.

At the 'minimal' end of the spectrum, health is defined in relation to disease, this being understood in strictly physical terms. Health, then, is the absence of physical disease or illness.

Towards the centre of the spectrum are concepts of health which are related to statistical norms for health in a given society. If disease is understood less in physical terms, and more in terms of sickness – deviation from a social norm – health is then understood as conformity to that social norm. For example, certain forms of obsessional behaviour are seen as socially unacceptable, and so 'unhealthy'.

Further along the spectrum still, we find the definition of health advocated by Freud, and others, that to be healthy means to be able to function well in society. Health, for Freud, is the capacity for work and enjoyment. If a person's capacity for work is diminished, and his or her capacity for pleasure impaired, that person is counted as ill.

The 'maximal' end of the spectrum of definitions is

exemplified by the now notorious definition of the World Health Organization (WHO): 'Health is a state of complete physical, mental and social well-being, not simply the absence of illness and disease.'

The lack of clarity in definitions of health can be illustrated further by the different ways in which the concept of health is often used, in relation both to physical and to mental life.

In physical terms, 'health' might refer to longevity. It might mean agility, or strength, or resistance to disease. What is the relationship between these? Is a person more healthy when one aspect of his or her being is exceptionally well developed? Or does health require all parts to be working in harmony?

In mental terms, the problems are even more marked. In *The Religious Experience*,[1] C. D. Batson and W. L. Ventis document at least seven working definitions of mental health from a survey of over fifty research papers:

1. Absence of mental illness, defined by identifiable symptoms of psychopathology;

2. Appropriate social behaviour, defined by the social group to which one belongs;

3. Freedom from worry and guilt (building on Freud's specification of the ability to love and to work as the hallmark of mental health, or Karen Horney's suggestion that self-hate, arising from a conception of an unattainable 'ideal self', is the root of neurotic conflict);

4. Personal competence and control, deriving from the psychologies of motivation;

5. Self-acceptance and self-actualization (humanistic psychology's interest in the ability freely to express one's true nature);

6. Personality unification, based on Allport's concept of the healthy, mature personality in terms of a unified and hierarchically organized personality structure;

7. Open-mindedness and flexibility – the capacity for change and adaptation.

Clearly, the definition of health is not a straightforward matter.

What do we need a definition of health for?

The confusion in defining health arises because of the failure to ask the prior question: What do we need a definition of health *for*? If our purpose in defining health is to advocate an ideal pattern of life for individuals or for society, which will make for the greatest happiness and sense of fulfilment of the greatest number, we will tend towards the maximal definition of the WHO. This is a goal, perhaps, towards which individuals and societies can aspire. If, however, we need a definition of health which can be applied in the allocation of limited healthcare resources, and our concern is to restrict our provision of medical resources to the basic essentials of what may be considered each person's right, or need, we will favour a minimal definition: medicine will be seen in terms of combating physical disabilities and disease.

We tend to work with a close association in our minds between 'health' and 'medical care'. This makes it all the more important to be clear what we are seeking a definition of health *for*. Too wide a definition will tend to 'medicalize' every aspect of life, and, because medical resources are necessarily limited, will inevitably lead to the sense that 'health' for all is some unattainable utopia. Too narrow a definition will lead to the restriction of medical care merely to physical bodily needs, whereas we are sure that 'health' involves more than the body. R. A. McCormick quotes the *New York Times* report of the surgeon whose kidney-transplanted recipient was undergoing anxiety and depression after his transplant: 'Well, I gave him a good kidney; I can't help what's wrong with his brain.'[2]

Our definition of health will depend on what we want a definition *for*.

Assumptions about human values

Our definition of health will also depend on the basic values which we assume, and our understanding of the purpose of human life. For underlying any of these above definitions are certain beliefs about what makes for the best in human life, certain value assumptions about what is good. And behind these are fundamental guiding metaphors about the significance of human life in this world. The understanding of what counts as healthy reflects a particular society's values, and the way human beings fit in with the demands of that society.

Freud worked with a mechanistic model of human life, in which pleasure was the greatest good. His definition of health naturally focused on the capacity for satisfaction in love and in work. It fits in with an industrial society whose central values are towards production and consumption. Jung's fundamental metaphor was of the union of opposites in a person's life: health for him was found in the individuation of the personal self. Maslow's hierarchy of human needs was related to his concept of 'self-actualization' as a human being's highest good. These reflect the common emphasis on the individual in post-Enlightenment society.

It is important to raise the question of the relationship between the value of health and other human goods. Some of the 'cults of health' seem to treat health as an absolute value. We need to ask, however, whether health is in fact to be seen as an absolute. At the point of fundamental assumptions about human goods and human needs is where a theology of health needs to begin. So a theology of health is integrally related to a theological anthropology.

A theological anthropology

Theological anthropology, or a theological understanding of what it is to be human, begins with Jesus Christ. He is the Normal Human Being, though of course in this fallen world is abnormal in being so. He is the one human being of whom it is said, 'He is the image of the invisible God' (Col. 1:15), and is presented in the pages of the New Testament as the one in whom all God's purposes for humanity are summed up and find their fulfilment. Jesus Christ is depicted as the one Genuinely Human Being, by reference to whom all other human life is seen as falling short of God's glory. If he is the Human Being, we are all Human Becomings, on the way to our true humanity, as that is found in relation to Jesus Christ. Such is the witness of the Bible.

Jesus Christ, however, does not easily fit into our definitions of normality. He does not belong to any clear social group. He was on occasion described as mad. In fact, some of his experiences may in our social terms be regarded as either pathological or at least socially unacceptable. From a Christian theological perspective, however, this should lead us to evaluate our contemporary culture in his light, rather than the other way round.

Let us enumerate some of the features of Jesus Christ's human life.

He recognized spiritual realities, and that eternal life is a gift to be received in relationship to God. He demonstrated the fulfilment of a life lived in communion with and dependence on God the Father, and not in the assertion of an individual human autonomy. He recognized the reality of sin, and that this present world is disordered and fallen, and in need of redemption, resurrection and re-creation. Jesus expressed his anger at the unnaturalness of death (as seen in his reactions at the grave of Lazarus) as an alien intrusion into God's world, and yet he accepted the sting of death on behalf of humankind in his own death on the cross. Jesus Christ experienced the depression and abandonment of alienation in his cry of dereliction from the cross, 'My God, why have you forsaken me?' By so doing he demonstrated unmistakably that wholeness is not always to be associated with happiness. Indeed, it is through suffering, pain and abandonment that salvation is achieved. His resurrection from the dead is a pointer towards the 'new creation': that God is making this disordered world new, and so this present world, and our human lives within it, are only 'on the way'.

Jesus Christ's life also illustrates the fact that human life encompasses many different dimensions and levels, all of which are important.

His incarnation as the Word made flesh sets a value on the importance of the *body*. Human life is embodied life. In contrast to some Greek understandings of human life, the body is not an evil part of our humanity to be subdued, not merely the prison house of the soul. No, the body is to be affirmed: anatomy, physiology and genetic make-up are all to be taken seriously as part of the goodness of God's creation.

Jesus Christ illustrates, too, the full range of human *emotions*, appropriately managed and used. He weeps, he rages, he snorts in indignation, he rejoices with those who rejoice, he celebrates at a wedding, he gets tired. The emotional life of our Lord indicates that emotions are to be taken seriously.

Jesus Christ based much of his self-understanding on the concept of the *will* of God. His will was to do the Father's will. The area of responsible moral choice is also part of the meaning of our humanity.

The *relational dimension* to human life is also vital in the life of Jesus. He made relationships of love with men and women. The affective dimensions of his sexuality are given appropriate expression in him. To be in relationship with another human person is to reflect something of the meaning of the image of the God who is a trinity of Persons in love and communication. Our well-being as human bearers of the divine image is found in personal communion, fellowship, mutual interdependence with other persons and with God.

Jesus also shows himself again and again *on the side of the poor*, the outcast, the prostitute, the tax gatherer, the sinner. He has come to save the lost. One aspect of true humanity is seen in attitudes and actions of compassion to the hungry who have no food, the thirsty who need drink, the person who needs shelter or clothing, the prisoner who needs to be visited. Wholeness and social justice belong together. The redemption which Jesus Christ has come to offer to the world, and to secure through his self-giving love, is a redemptive justice which is concerned with social conditions of human living as much as with individual personal needs.

The basic Hebraic conception of humanness, however, is not a plurality of 'body, plus mind, plus will', but a psychophysical *unity*. We are embodied souls and ensouled bodies, without distinction.

Having taken our bearings from the life of Jesus Christ, whom Luther called the 'Proper Man', we can now fill out ten further aspects of a theological anthropology.

1. According to the creation story at the beginning of the Bible, human life is intended to be lived in a satisfying physical environment, and a fulfilling social context. In Genesis 2, God put the man in a garden to cultivate and protect it. The garden had trees which were 'pleasing to the eye and good for food'. The physical environment for human life is important, and it is part of God's commission to humankind to cultivate and protect that environment so that life can flourish. Health is enhanced through an appropriately facilitating environment, and diminished through an unsatisfying one.

2. It was not good that man should be alone, so God gave *Ishshah* to match *Ish* in his eminence and his need, a helper 'like-opposite' him as his equal and his complement. Neither man nor woman is thereafter complete without the other.

3. The image of God in us is distorted and marred by sin, which causes alienation between ourselves and God, between ourselves and one another, between ourselves and the rest of the natural order, and within our own beings. This world is a fallen world, still 'in Adam', but not back in Eden. The story of Cain and Abel illustrates the destructiveness of competitive jealousy within social division (Gn. 4). The story of the Tower of Babel illustrates the fracture of human communities when social structures are set up without reference to God (Gn. 11). The eighth-century prophets, particularly Amos and Micah, forcefully underline the inhumanity of unjust social structures, the powerlessness of poverty, and God's will for social as well as

individual 'righteousness'. God has shown us what is good: 'To act justly, to love mercy and to walk humbly with your God' (Mi. 6:8).

4. As a gift of grace, Christ offers us a renewed humanity in which the image of God is being restored. In him there is a reversal of the effects of the Fall, spiritually, socially, personally, and psychologically. We can be 'new creations' in Christ. We are given the fellowship of the Holy Spirit, and are baptized into the communion of the Christian church. Even for those who do not acknowledge God, his 'common grace' is at work in the world, restraining the full effects of sin and disorder. We may regard medical care as part of the common grace of God.

5. Full, total, human well-being – indeed the renewal of the whole creation – is God's purpose and promise. 'Salvation' is a wide-ranging word, often meaning 'healing'. It is used of healing disease (Mk. 10:52), curing leprosy (Lk. 17:19), and restoring the withered hand (Mk. 3:4–5). It is used of deliverance from evil spirits: the demoniac is 'saved' (Lk. 8:36). It is used of the disciples in trouble on the boat (Mt. 8:25). It is used of Zaccheus when Jesus put right his business priorities (Tyndale on Lk. 19:9 reads: 'Today "health" has come to this house').

6. Salvation/healing at all levels of life is God's work, sometimes through intermediaries. 'Yahweh who [gives] you healing' (Ex. 15:26, JB); and 'Yahweh-Peace' (Jdg. 6:24, JB) is made known in Christ (Eph. 2:14), and is at work in grace, in Christ, through the Spirit. 'By his wounds you have been healed' (1 Pet. 2:24). God's healing work is to restore communion between men and women and God (2 Cor. 5:19), between men and women with each other (Eph. 2:11ff.), and between men and women and their natural environment (Rom. 8:19ff.) His work is also to restore communion in the social contexts of life (the Household Codes of the epistles illustrate the significance of the gospel for the ordering of social life), and within individual people (Paul prays that 'the God of peace [may] himself sanctify you wholly; and may your spirit and soul and body be kept sound and blameless' (1 Thes. 5:23, RSV).

Wholeness of life is synonymous with 'the measure of the stature of the fulness of Christ' (Eph. 4:13, RSV).

7. The social structures within which human life is lived contribute to peoples' sense of well-being. Not only so, but the social structures which we employ are intended to reflect the nature of the new society which God is building as the kingdom of his Son. The community of creation is being restored. The New Testament shows how the patterns of social life among Christian people are intended to reflect the nature of what God is doing by his gospel. Thus when the truth dawns that Jew and Gentile are no longer at enmity, but that through Christ they are made one, the pattern of their social relationships (Gal. 2) has to reflect this change. Justice is the social expression of neighbour-love. Just as the eighth-century prophets of the Old Testament, like Amos and Micah, proclaimed the need for justice to roll down like waters and righteousness like an everflowing stream (Am. 5:24, RSV), so the New Testament concentration on neighbour-love assumes that social structures will need to be rethought in the light of the gospel.

8. In Christian experience, individually and corporately, there is always a distinction between Now and Not Yet. Salvation has a *past* reference (Eph. 2:8), is a *present* experience (1 Cor. 1:18) and is a *future* hope (Rom. 5:9). God's work of renewal, resurrection and recreation, begins now, but is not promised in its fulness until the new heaven and the new earth. We are only ever 'on the way'. If Christ is the Human Being, we are all still Human Becomings, on the way towards wholeness. To be made whole is a dynamic process of growth and change. We must not treat life in this world as an absolute.

9. The writers in the New Testament indicate that it is appropriate to pray for, and therefore to work for, physical health (*cf.* 3 Jn. 2; Jas. 5:14; 2 Cor. 12:8), although there is no evidence for universal physical health in the New Testament.[3] In this prayer and work, the New Testament authors are reflecting the importance which healing played in the life of Jesus. His works of healing are evidences of the presence of the kingdom of God, signs of

God's power, and a summons to the life of faith.

10. We need to note the point made by R. A. Lambourne, in *Community, Church and Healing*,[4] that the healings of Jesus are depicted in the gospels as community events. The occasions of healing are primarily seen as signs of the kingdom, and are acted parables which were intended to provoke a response from those who witnessed them. Some saw in Jesus' healings only the work of Beelzebul; others saw the work of the Holy Spirit. Each event provoked a response from the witnesses. As S. Pattison comments: 'The healing functioned as concrete judgement of the Kingdom on actual earthly communities.'[5] The healing work of Jesus thus has a challenging, judging and social dimension. A theology of health needs to be set in the context of a theology of the demands of the kingdom of God.

Health and shalom

We can attempt to summarize where the above discussion of basic theological parameters is taking us, with the proposition that in theological terms, 'health' is part of what the Bible means by shalom.

Often translated 'peace' in the Old Testament, shalom means much more than the absence of conflict. Shalom means wholeness, well-being, vigour and vitality in all the dimensions of human life. 'Health' is clearly part of shalom, as can be illustrated by the numerous times in the Old Testament when shalom is bracketed together with a Hebrew word translated 'health' or 'healing'.[6] Thus, the vision of peace in Isaiah 2:1–5 (which could almost stand as a definition of shalom) is set in contrast to the sickness of the nation (1:5–6), its idolatry (2:6–22), and social injustice (3:13–15), which bring the judgment that the Lord will not be a healer (3:7b).

Jeremiah writes, 'We hoped for *peace*, but no good has come, for a time of *healing*, but there was only terror' (8:15).

The suffering Servant brings justice to the nations (Is. 42:1–4), and suffers for the healing and atonement of the people: 'Upon him was the chastisement that made us whole' (shalom), and with his stripes we are healed' (Is. 53:5, RSV).

The concepts of shalom and health are linked in some of the Psalms, and also in the New Testament.[7]

In the synoptic gospels, the coming of the kingdom of Christ is depicted as a conflict with the 'Prince of this world', and the exorcisms and healings of Jesus demonstrate that he is the Messiah, anointed to 'preach good news to the poor', ... 'to proclaim freedom for the prisoners, and recovery of sight for the blind, to release the oppressed' (Lk. 4:18–19).

Jesus Christ, in other words, is the bringer of peace, shalom, wholeness, health. In biblical terms, health, therefore, is a *holistic* concept. It is not only the absence of disorder at all levels of life and relationship, it is also all that God gives for human well-being in all levels of human life. When the Lord brings shalom, there is prosperity (Ps. 72:1–7); there is a healthy relationship with God (Is. 57:19); there is conciliation between people (Gn. 26:29); there is contentedness (Gn; 15:15; Ps. 4:8). When the peace of the Lord is present, there are good relationships between nations and men and women (1 Ch. 12:17–18). There is a personal and social dimension to shalom: 'Seek the welfare (shalom) of the city where I have sent you into exile', writes Jeremiah, 'Pray to the LORD on its behalf, for in its welfare you will find your welfare' (Je. 29:7, RSV).

In summary so far, the Bible points us to a holistic and dynamic concept of health, which covers individual and social, physical and mental, temporal and spiritual life. It reminds us, however, that wholeness, in this sense, is only ever partially enjoyed now. It is a process of change which comes to its fulness only in the new heaven and the new earth (*cf.* 2 Pet. 3:11–13).

Sickness, sin and death

We need to take note at this point of Stephen Pattison's stringent comment:

> I am tempted to suggest that wholeness is a concept which is only really used by those of us who are so far removed from the real fight for health and healing in daily life that we can claim to see the world in terms of ideal universal patterns rather than in terms of the very unsatisfactory specifics provided by the 'worm's-eye view'.

He asks where talk of wholeness fits into the daily reality confronted by patients and staff in an underfunded National Health Service? 'And what is the real value of the term for the dispossessed peoples of the world who suffer most from the diseases and disorders of the present time?'[8]

Of course we need to hold the biblical vision of shalom in tension with the harsh realities of struggle in this world. And the biblical theme which covers this is 'sin', which is expressed in alienation between human beings and God, between themselves, and between them and their environment. Integral to a biblical view of health is also its insistence on the reality of sin and the power of death.

Sometimes a person's physical ill-health is caused by that person's sin. Miriam (Nu. 12) and Uzziah (2 Ch. 26:19) come in that category. It is the assumption of Job's counsellors, and the assumption held by several people in the New Testament (*cf.* Jn. 9:2). However, the book of Job, and Jesus' reply to his disciples (Jn. 9:3f.; *cf.* also Lk. 13:2), make clear that we may not make too direct an equation of specific sin with specific sickness.

Sometimes ill-health is caused by others' sins. The sins of the fathers are visited on the children to the third and fourth generation (Ex. 20:5). Sometimes the cause is unclear within the terms of this physical world (Job).

The cleansing from sin and the restoration of well-being in a person's relationship to God may alleviate depression

(Ps. 77), and may have physical benefits also (Pr. 3:7–8; *cf.* the healing of the paralysed man, Mk. 2:10).

Sometimes sickness comes through lack of care for the body (*cf.* 1 Tim. 5:23), sometimes through improper or inadequate use of the means of grace (1 Cor. 11:29–30).

Sickness functions as a messenger of death. It reminds us of the frailty and mortality of life this side of heaven. It points us to the fact of death, that we will all die, and that our concepts of salvation, wholeness and health have to reckon with the inevitability of death. Sickness can also function as a messenger of the gospel, pointing us beyond the rule of death to the necessity and gift of eternal life in Christ. God then can be understood as 'allowing' illness (*cf.* Jb. 1), even 'sending' sickness (Ex. 15:23–26). Sickness can point back to things that need to be put right in a person's past (*cf.* Ps. 38:3–4); it can lead to meditation and care for the future (*cf.* Elihu's word to Job: Jb. 33:19ff.). Suffering, pain and conflict can themselves bring healing. In the Old Testament, Yahweh is the Lord of sickness and of healing, (Ex. 15:26); all aspects of human life find their health in him. To seek other healers in place of Yahweh is futile (2 Ch. 16:12), though God does work through medicine.

In the Wisdom literature from the second century BC, the apocryphal book of Ecclesiasticus (38:1–15, RSV) outlines what may well then have been a common view, that medical skill is God's gift.

> *Honour the physician with the honour due him*
> *for healing comes from the Most High,*
> > *and he will receive a gift from the king.*
> *The skill of the physician lifts up his head,*
> > *and in the presence of great men he is admired.*
> *The Lord created medicines from the earth,*
> > *and a sensible man will not despise them . . .*
> *By them he heals and takes away pain;*
> > *the pharmacist makes of them a compound . . .*
>
> *My son, when you are sick do not be negligent,*
> > *but pray to the Lord, and he will heal you.*

> *Give up your faults and direct your hands aright,*
>   *and cleanse your heart from all sin . . .*
> *And give the physician his place, . . . for the Lord created*
>   *him;*
>   *let him not leave you, for there is need of him.*
> *There is a time when success lies in the hands of*
>   *physicians,*
>   *for they too will pray to the Lord that he should grant*
>   *them success in diagnosis*
>   *and in healing, for the sake of preserving life.*
> *He who sins before his Maker,*
>   *may he fall into the hands of a physician.*

Commenting on this passage, H. W. Wolff remarks:

> Here the medical profession is viewed with sober
> realism. The doctor has his wisdom and skill from
> God, just as medicines are gifts of the Creator
> from the earth. He can arrive at the right diag-
> nosis, can relieve pain, and perhaps preserve life.
> But his gifts have their limitations and he does not
> always have them at his disposal. So he himself,
> like the sick person, is dependent on prayer.
> Moreover, it can be a punishment to fall into the
> hands of a doctor. God and the physician are
> therefore seen in conjunction with one another in
> curious and multifarious ways.[9]

Because of sin, and the ever-present rule of death, we
need an approach to health which is consistent with a
theology of frailty, suffering, disease and mortality.
Health, like life in general, is not eternal but is limited. Like
life, it is entrusted to human beings by God, but does not
belong to us. Health is to be affirmed and willed by us, but
not absolutely; health, like life, is on loan from God.

Wholeness and holiness

Health is not the greatest value. Although a person who fears the Lord and turns away from evil will find it 'healing to your flesh and refreshment to your bones' (Pr. 3:8), it is the pursuit of wisdom herself that is to be prized highly (Pr. 4:1, 8, *etc.*). The Wisdom of God is that knowledge of God and his ways which tunes a person in to the ways of God in the world, and enables fellowship with him. Wisdom enables us to *live* – and to cope. Throughout the Bible, the fundamental command of the covenant is that we should 'be holy, as God is holy' (Lv. 19:2; 1 Pet. 1:15), and that involves ordering each aspect of life into line with God's character (Lv. 19). This ordering normally will include care for health (as Leviticus also makes clear), but health is to serve the quest for holiness.

No doubt in the new heaven and the new earth, wholeness of personal life and holiness of character will be one and the same. But in this life, there can be holiness without wholeness, and 'wholeness' in some aspects of life, without holiness. Both are important tasks in the journey of faith, but holiness takes priority in the biblical mind.

The dynamic of faith

'Wisdom', as we understand the term from the Wisdom literature (Job, Proverbs, Ecclesiastes) is 'helping people to cope'. It gives an outlook on the world within which the uncertainties and frailties of ordinary human living can be managed and lived with. This is part of the meaning of faith. Faith is frequently not concerned with certainties, with successes, with achievement, but rather is the strength given by God for us to cope with uncertainties, disappointments and apparent failure.

If Jesus Christ is not only God for us, but Man for us, he is, in T. F. Torrance's phrase, the True Believer. He is the faithful one, and faith, for him, led him to Gethsemane, to Calvary, to the cry of dereliction ('My God, why . . .?'). As we noted before, it is only through suffering, pain, and abandonment that salvation is achieved. The fulness of resurrection-life comes by way of the vulnerability of the crucified God.

It is because of this that the New Testament sometimes places an unexpectedly high value on suffering ('Consider it pure joy . . .': Jas. 1:2; suffering produces endurance, character, hope: Rom. 5:2ff.). Our sufferings can be a share in the sufferings of Christ (Phil. 3:10). They can be part of our journey to wholeness.

This approach to faith is dynamic, moving, concerned with growth, development and change. Faith is a journey of discovery, and movement towards the fulness of Christ. Our understanding of wholeness, of shalom, and therefore of health, must likewise be dynamic. It is more concerned with attitude, and with the development of character, than with a state of being or well-being.

In summary, the biblical picture of health, therefore, is a holistic one in which all aspects of life are involved, a dynamic one which acknowledges that we are part of a salvation-history process in God's dealings with the world, yet a limited one which acknowledges that perfect shalom, perfect health, is not possible this side of heaven.

A look back at the WHO definition of health

The above approach stands in contrast to contemporary definitions of health which concentrate on the individual, to the exclusion of his or her social or environmental context. It stands in contrast to contemporary definitions of health which are concerned only with the physical and bodily, and regard the mental and emotional aspects of life as of secondary importance. It stands in contrast to contemporary definitions of health which ignore the significance of a person's relationship – and a society's relationship – with God. It takes very seriously the importance of health as part of the work of God in people and in societies, but it does not make physical well-being into an absolute. Health is not the supreme value. The above approach stands in contrast to static definitions of health which concentrate on a 'state of well-being', rather than with the dynamic and changing character of the whole person.

In the light of this, the World Health Organization definition is both too limited and too broad. It is too limited, because it makes no reference to a person's spiritual progress as part of the meaning of health. It is also too limited by concentrating on a 'state of well-being', which tends to equate the human *person* with human *health*, and fails to see human health as a constantly changing part of, but not the whole of, human life. Health becomes not only a human right to which everyone is entitled, but also a 'state' of well-being which does not allow for the changing dynamics of the *strength* to be human itself.

On the other hand, the WHO definition is too broad because in failing to recognize the inevitability of death, and the ambiguity of the fallen world, it ends in an idealistic utopian vision which is not attainable in this life. It offers 'the utopia of a life without suffering, happiness without pain, and a community without conflicts . . .'.[10] Yet, as we have said, suffering can be redemptive, suffering can be part of the strength to live healthily.

A working definition of health

We need to narrow this discussion down towards a working definition of health for the purposes of medicine and healthcare delivery in this world. It needs to be narrow enough to depict medical responsibility realistically, and not to be utopian; it needs to be broad enough to recognize that health and sickness are aspects of the whole person.

The Catholic theologian Bernard Häring has made one approach:

> A comprehensive understanding of human health includes the greatest possible harmony of all

man's forces and energies, the highest possible
spiritualisation of man's bodily reality, and the
finest embodiment of the spiritual. True health is
revealed in the self-actualisation of persons who
have attained the freedom that marshals all their
talents and energies for the fulfilment of their
total human vocation.[11]

More simply, Karl Barth regards health as 'the power to
be as man'.[12] Following him, Moltmann puts it even more
clearly: '*health . . . is the strength to be human*' (my italics).[13]

Moltmann's definition needs some clarification. Taken
on its own and out of a theological context of the meaning
of humanness, the definition would not be enough. It
would suggest that to be lacking in health is to be lacking in
the strength to be fully human, and that could suggest that
only healthy people are fully human. We would need to
ensure that this definition is seen in the context of our
discussion of humanness. This, as we have indicated, is
understood in terms of our relationship to Christ who is
the image of God, and of ourselves as beings 'on the way' to
full humanness as our lives are growing into maturity in
him. Furthermore, we would need to recognize that there
is some ambiguity in the meaning of 'strength'. Does
'strength' refer to some capacity we have within ourselves,
something that is subject to our will and our choice, or is
'strength' something that is given to us, by God, or by
others? Is the responsibility for finding this strength – the
responsibility for health, that is – ours, or God's, or
society's? These questions are part of the current debate
about responsibility for health within our society. With
these caveats, however, Moltmann's definition seems a
good pointer to the meaning of health: the strength to be
human.

In these terms, sickness, then, is the impairment of this
strength, crippling and weakening a person. It may be an
impairment which is physical (bacterial infection), emotional (stress), relational (deep-seated hurts from the past,
or inherited patterns of belief or behaviour), social (certain

social and economic structures may maintain ill-health through, for example, the poverty trap), or environmental (air, water, or noise pollution, high-rise housing). It may be to do with lifestyle, habits or lack of personal care (diet, smoking, recreation, substance abuse, alcohol, sleep patterns, commuting, factory conditions, and the like).

If health is 'the strength to be human', a person can have healthy or morbid attitudes to his states of health *or* sickness. It can be displayed in a person's capacity for happiness *and* suffering, in his or her acceptance of life's joys *and* the grief of death.[14]

Moltmann's conclusion is worth quoting in full:

> If health as a state of general well-being is declared to be the supreme value in a human life and in a society, this really implies a morbid attitude to health. Being human is equated with being healthy. This leads to the suppression of illness in the individual life, and means that the sick are pushed out of the life of society and kept out of the public eye. To turn the idea of health into an idol in this way is to rob the human being of the true strength of his humanity. Every serious illness which he has to suffer plunges him into a catastrophe, robs him of his confidence in life, and destroys his sense of his own value.
>
> But if we understand health as *the strength to be human* [my italics], then we make being human more important than the state of being healthy. Health is not the meaning of human life. On the contrary, a person has to prove the meaning he has found in his own life in conditions of health *and* sickness. Only what can stand up to both health *and* sickness, and ultimately to living *and* dying, can count as a valid definition of what it means to be human.[15]

Many of the contemporary 'cults of health' are forms of idolatry which actually produce what they set out to remove: fear of illness. An approach which, while positively encouraging the importance of seeking the strength to be human, also faces the reality of frailty and death, liberates us to see health as a servant to our humanity. To be set free from the idolatry of health opens us to the possibility of a more fully human life – a life which includes the creativity of vulnerability, and the possibilities of a faith which holds us in life's uncertainties, and also the gift of life through death in the presence of God.

Responsibility for health

If human life is God's gift, and health is the strength to be human, then a person's right to health is a basic human right, which lays on each person for him or herself and for others the duty of respecting and facilitating health as well as life. Just as God may withhold life, so he may withhold health – or at least withhold health in a physical sense, so that a person may grow in other senses (*cf.* Paul's thorn in the flesh). But we cannot make that judgment for one another. It is not for one human being to withhold, or damage, the health of another. Rather there is laid on us an obligation to ensure as far as possible that we and others are able to live healthy lives.

The following will need to be borne in mind:

a. Our theology of the *body*, as the temple of the Holy Spirit, requires us to take responsibility for bodily care (nourishment, clothing, hygiene, housing, recreation, sports, sleep, and appropriate use of medication – while avoiding what Häring calls the 'seduction of the drug industry').

b. Our theology of *persons in relation* requires us to take responsibility for the fact that 'it is not good to be alone', either emotionally or physically. In our individualized post-Enlightenment culture, we need to emphasize very clearly the importance of community, fellowship, friendship, and relational growth. A gospel of grace, forgiveness, a truth which sets free, and a love which casts out fear, oblige us to ensure that our fellow human beings are given resources for personal relational well-being. They require us to take seriously, and combat, the social structures which may impede health.

c. Our theology of the *environment* derives in part from the mandate given to mankind in creation, and is reinforced in the 'protest' of the thorns and thistles to the sin of mankind (Gn. 3), asserting the significance of the natural order, and that humankind must still cultivate and protect it though now with struggle and pain. This theology obliges us to take seriously the implications for health of environmental pollution, ecological devastation, and climatic changes. There is need for popular understanding of the need for clean drinking water, the avoidance of toxic gases in the air, the enforcement of speed limits, and the like.

d. Our theology of *government* sees it as a limited and temporary provision of God for the ordering of human society in justice and righteousness, as far as possible within the ambiguity and compromise of a fallen world. This view will require us to take seriously the task of sharing health-care resources, so that each may benefit according to need. This is at once a *global* question, related to economic structures and international co-operation (the sharing of the rich North with the poor South); a *national* question (in the allocation of priorities in national budgets between health-care and other social priorities); a *local* question (shall money be spent on geriatric care, or kidney machines? Who may benefit when not all can?); and a *medical and social* question (are resources to be allocated on the basis of quality of life judgments, medical indications, random distribution, or what?).

Clearly, the spectrum of political opinion stretches from those who see government as a minimal provision for the needs only of personal freedoms (law and order enforcement), to those who see government as a maximal provision for benefits as well as freedoms (equality of opportunity, and an equitable share of available resources). From the concern of Amos for social justice, the constant insistence that God is on the side of the poor, the oppressed, the widow and the orphan, and the way shalom is so often linked with justice in society, many Christians believe that it is part of government responsibility to ensure that available resources are equitably distributed in society.

e. Our theology of *sanctification* reminds us that 'the road to holiness is paved with genuine prudent concern for health ... and a humble readiness to accept the human predicament of illness'.[16] We are called, for ourselves and for one another, to ensure as far as is possible that the personal, social, economic and environmental conditions are such that each has the opportunity to grow in health towards maturity in Christ. We do so recognizing that God may purpose differing priorities for different people, and differing priorities for one person at varying stages of his or her life journey. We shall remember that God sometimes withholds physical healing in order to heal us in other ways first, and that perfect health is not promised us this side of heaven. So we shall have an eye to that day when 'there will be no more death or mourning or crying or pain, for the old order of things has passed away' (Rev. 21:4). The leaves of the tree of life, the prophet tells us, are 'for the healing of the nations' (Rev. 22:2).

References

1 C. D. Batson and W. L. Ventis, *The Religious Experience* (Oxford University Press, 1982), pp. 211ff.

2 R. A. McCormick, *How Brave a New World?* (SCM Press, 1981), p. 43.

3 *Cf.* Timothy: 1 Tim. 5:23; Trophimus: 2 Tim. 4:20; Epaphroditus: Phil. 2:27; and Paul: 2 Cor. 12:7f.

4 R. A. Lambourne, *Community, Church and Healing* (Darton, Longman & Todd, 1963; repr. Arthur James, 1987).

5 S. Pattison, *Alive and Kicking* (SCM Press, 1989), p. 80.

6 *Cf.* W. M. Swartley, 'Shalom and Healing', unpublished paper.

7 Lk. 10:5–9; Acts 10:36–38; Mk. 5.24–34; Heb. 12:13–14; 1 Pet. 2:13 – 3:12.

8 S. Pattison, *op. cit.*, p. 77.
9 H. W. Wolff, *Anthropology of the Old Testament* (SCM Press, 1974), p. 147.
10 J. Moltmann, *God in Creation* (SCM Press, 1985), p. 272.
11 B. Häring, *Free and Faithful in Christ* (St Paul Publications, 1981), 3, p. 48; *cf. idem, Medical Ethics* (St Paul Publications, ²1974), p. 154.
12 K. Barth, *Church Dogmatics* (T. & T. Clark, 1961) III/4, p. 357.
13 J. Moltmann, *op. cit.*, p. 273.
14 *Ibid.*
15 *Ibid.*
16 B. Häring, *Medical Ethics*, p. 157.

Chapter Two

A CHRISTIAN ECONOMICS AND SOCIOLOGY OF HEALTH

Alan Storkey

Lecturer, Oak Hill Theological College, London

What is an economics and sociology of health?

If a biblical understanding of health involves the full well-being of a person before God, then far more is involved in healthcare than remedial medical work. To be healthy involves good work, rest, nourishment and shelter, and it requires the kind of relationships in family, marriage, politics and community which allow harmonious living. The practice in many cultures of sending young fit men off to fight wars has often proved very unhealthy!

The biblical understanding is also not individualistic. My love for my neighbour is to be as my love for myself, for God is no respecter of persons. Such love involves equity in economic relationships and in the social care which is given and received. This does not happen at a direct personal level only, but also through the structural principles which from the time of Moses onwards are spelt out in God's concern for justice within and among the nations. As Jesus lived among the people he directly healed, fed the hungry, restored relationships, put worry to rest, met violence with shalom, lightened economic burdens and attacked the enslaving power of mammon. In the light of this open and comprehensive response to human needs we need to re-evaluate some of the partial and reductionist views of health which have gained weight in modern Western cultures.

In some Western cultures especially the meaning of health has been defined largely in applied biological terms by a medical professional group which promotes health care in terms of drugs, operations and other technical developments. This medical misconception of health, narrowing the full Christian conception of the strength to be human, is one from which this book fundamentally departs, and its limitations need to be fully exposed.

First, natural created processes in our bodies are still overwhelmingly the route by which healing takes place. God has given us all structures of restoration and re-creation which continually work in our bodies to refresh and re-energize us. These systems of health remain the ones within which medical science operates in a supplementary role, and respect for them is the *sine qua non* of good medical science.

Second, the sources of illness and disease are personal, not just biological. Stress illnesses and other psychosomatic ones show clear links between the psyche and patterns of illness. Overwork, malnutrition, overeating, poor sanitation, road accidents, poor water and other economic factors are obviously causes of a very high proportion of illness. War, criminal activity and population displacement generate many more sick people, and broken families, destructive relationships, unloving sexual activity, status and social power leave many people ill and uncared for. Relations between the old, young and middle-aged also involve a range of health problems. Thus, we see that the development of illness is a far wider phenomenon than being merely biological and involves the full-orbed life of persons living before God. In the face of this a conception of health and sickness which is biological is dangerously flawed and inadequate, failing to address these other areas of life in their fulness.

Jesus was and is the full personal healer, concerned on the cross with his grieving mother, forgiving sins and healing legs, restoring outcasts and freeing those in bondage. If this full personal view of health is the correct one, then the economics and sociology of health have a key role in understanding what is important in sustaining the health of the people. In this chapter we shall recognize that a high proportion of, indeed even most, human sickness is rooted in the failures of our economic and social lives. But our understanding and action in these areas need to be opened up and shaped by God's revelation of what economic and social life mean, for it rapidly becomes clear that contemporary Western conceptions are creating more health problems than they solve.

1. Christian health economics

Health economics has traditionally been defined in certain circumscribed ways. Often it has been seen as involving economic decision-making in the allocation and use of medical resources. These choices are important. Every nurse, operating theatre, bed and drug involves a commitment of economic resources, and often these commitments have to be weighed against alternative uses. Thus, the decrease in the number of hospital beds weighed against the increase in numbers treated reflects an economizing process. But the process is wider than this. For decades doctors have been aware that early diagnosis is one of the best aids to efficient as well as effective treatment. Yet although even this area of concern has wide implications, the tendency recently in American management philosophies is to try to narrow the framework in which the issues are considered. They have attempted to reformulate these processes of economizing in accounting terms borrowed from some of the traditions of neo-classical economics. We shall consider what is involved in this move later. The fundamental point, however, is that a Christian perspective on this area should not become tied down to a narrow conception which forecloses its ability to see the deeper range of issues which actually arise. For example, one of the most important medical resources is the understanding and diagnostic ability ordinary people have of their own health. A person who knows when to go to the doctor or hospital can save a lot of resources. Health education in schools is therefore an important part of this allocative process, yet often health is ignored or downplayed in the taught curriculum because it is defined out of the framework.

Health economics is also seen in terms of choices which involve allocation of resources and demands between the health services and other sectors of the economy. Normally this is seen as a political issue to be expressed in terms of the proportion of Gross National Product (GNP) which is given to medical services. This view again defines the issue too narrowly. Healthcare is not just a matter for government, but for all the other economic institutions which shape our lives. Firms should care for the safety of their workers and the healthiness of their products, schools for the physical fitness of children, professional groups should take care with the stress levels of their members, families with the rest, diet and cleanliness of children and adults. Thus, for example, the promotion of the motor car downplays the effects of unfitness, accidents, pollution, noise, stress – all major causes of illness – in favour of other priorities. It is often a disservice to health which is carried out through government, market and community decisions. The allocation of resources to health involves more than government. Companies, markets, financial institutions, communities and families are all involved, and the underlying consideration is whether concern for the health of others is reflected in all our economic decisions and activities. Thus, there is almost no area of our daily economic lives from which issues of health can be excluded, and the real issue is therefore why in Western and poor economies health, and especially the health of others, is so little valued. In many poor countries the answer is plain; it is the shortage of food, water, shelter, sanitation, knowledge and healthy work. In the West the answers are more paradoxical.

Thus, a Christian analysis of the economics of health does not begin with an abstract body of analysis, which stands in its own right, to which questions of health are added like limpets. Rather it recognizes the value of health in all human lives as part of the economic stewardship which God calls us to exercise. Our economic valuations should, therefore, reflect issues of health – both our own and that of all other people – in an integral sense. Daily evidence emerges of how intimately related are our economic lifestyles and our health; it reflects the deeper understanding of Jesus who knew that all of our lives cohere in our relationship with God.

2. Health and the poor economies

Epidemiological studies across nations and over time lead to the conclusion that diet, drinking supplies, sanitation, clothing, exercise, personal hygiene, heating, ventilation and work patterns are the areas where most of the important issues of health occur, in comparison with which treatment in hospitals is relatively insignificant. This conclusion is still irrefutably close to the poorer countries of the world, where famine, malnutrition, poor water supplies, sanitation, fatigue, overcrowding and poor working conditions generate many of the illnesses which people suffer. Health is here primarily an economic pandemic, and the question is: How is it to be solved? Sometimes the answer is seen in terms of economic development or massive medical aid, but both these responses fail to get to grips with the way health is rooted in our economic lives. When economic development means pollution, powdered baby milk, shanty towns, agricultural collapse and migrant labour, often health suffers. Just as in the early nineteenth century

43

laissez-faire economic development often made the lot of the urban masses worse in terms of life expectancy than that of the rural poor, so economic development *per se* cannot be trusted. And those who are involved in medical aid know how much bigger than their response the problem is they face. How does a Christian see through this dilemma?

One deep problem is the way in which the health of the poor has been valued so cheaply through Western trading terms, patterns of investment, colonial and multinational control, technical and military domination. The West has often persuaded the economies of the poor to purchase military and private consumption goods which are inappropriate to their health needs. The answer to these problems lies in changes of Western response which go far deeper than an expansion of the present inadequate levels of aid. It involves, for example, a willingness to stop pushing the expansion of the private motor car because it is inappropriate to the healthy development of those countries. It means radical patterns of international debt cancellation and exchange rate support and a closing down of much of the Western arms trade.

Other problems arise from the gross inequalities of wealth and income, often held in position by military dictators or close oligarchies, which leave large sections of the population without the resources which they need to steward their lives and health. Often the exercise of control and power wastes resources through armies, policing, security, conflict and destruction. Here the lack of Christian principles of meekness, distribution, freedom and non-control means that economies are screwed up into patterns which generate poor health. In Ethiopia, Sudan, Cambodia, Bangladesh, Nicaragua, Afghanistan and other countries internal wars have often hindered aid and health programmes disastrously. These countries need to learn the lesson which permeates the books of Moses. It is when a nation distributes its resources to allow all of its citizens to exercise stewardship and have the means to contribute to the welfare of others that a nation prospers. Seriously imperfect though it is, the relatively equal distribution of resources, including education and training, is the backbone of Western economic development. Health therefore involves a radical redirection of resources and organization to empower ordinary people to develop healthy lives.

The understanding which the poor have of themselves needs also to grow out from slavery to foreign traders, property controllers, mass employers and the fatalism of the past into a full awareness of their value before God. Lessons of self-respect and mutual care, freedom from defeatism and the mores of the past, growth into maturity and wisdom of a kind different from that of the West, need to be absorbed from Jesus Christ. There needs to be a respect for the body as God's handiwork which allows patterns of superstition, Western and traditional magic, asceticism, fatalism and defeat to be sloughed off. There need to be patterns of personal care, hygiene, diet, fitness, cleanliness, use of space, waste handling and medical care which are learned by communities and allow neighbours to love one another in health and in sickness. These transformations are deep, but already many indigenous and missionary Christians have allowed them to take root. These revolutions of outlook are already underway. Perhaps out of respect for Western medical models they are not proceeding with the confidence which they should engender.

3. Health and the rich economies

Most Western economies have been able to some extent to meet these basic needs for a majority of their populations, although the idea that they have been superceded is grossly wrong. Ten, twenty, or thirty per cent of many Western populations suffer from levels of poverty which undermine their ability to live properly. There is, however, a range of other health problems that are Western in origin, which grow out of the structure and economic lifestyle promoted in Western economies. These are, of course, also being exported to the cosmopolitan centres of poorer nations, but their meaning is to be found in the affluent West.

The problem arises through production, investment,

sales and consumption which is undertaken for private profit or benefit, but which does not take into account financially the costs associated with the process. These costs are located with health and medical services and with the individuals and families who suffer.

Heart attacks are a matter of diet, smoking, drinking water, alcohol, exercise, and stress which is usually job-related. Cancer can be caused by consumer goods which are heavily marketed and addictive. Or again it is common in Western countries for bits of metal to travel very fast along highways colliding with one another and mashing up human beings in the process. Often the most sophisticated techniques in hospitals cannot repair the crude damage done to the injured or dying. Or again, there is probably a link between additives in food and patterns of allergy which are becoming increasingly common. These examples, and there are many more which could be cited, show how much the basic pattern of health and sickness is generated from people's wider economic activity and the way these costs are ignored or downplayed by those who make the crucial decisions. The source of the problem is clear. It is the economism of much Western economic decision-making which says that if options are viable in terms of private accounting costs, in a closed self-interested mode of calculation, then they are justified. Not surprisingly, blind self-interest produces casualties in others. The solution is no less clear. Justice requires not only patterns of individual compensation, but also the transfer of costs from those who presently suffer them to the economic activity which generates them. Thus tobacco, alcohol and petrol should carry taxes which represent the costs they generate in terms of hospital and other medical care, loss of earnings, pollution, noise, vandalism and physical destruction of property. If petrol costs doubled, the health of the nation would substantially improve.

There is another dimension of this issue which, although simple and obvious, needs highlighting. The relationship between health and economic life is reciprocal. Poor health impairs economic stewardship. People with meagre diets who are sick, cannot work efficiently. Many have had their effective worklife reduced through industrial injury. Others are too cold or hot to work effectively. Others, through overconsumption of alcohol and drugs, drastically reduce their ability to work. Without suggesting that the primary concern in any area of health is that people should be able to function as effective workers, the 'health efficiency' of the population is clearly very significant. Although this is an overwhelming problem in poor countries, also in affluent ones there are many who are unable to work effectively through overweight, stress, addictive patterns, alcohol, lack of rest and other factors. Every night millions watch television too late to be healthily awake to work the next day. They coast along in their work and the economy suffers.

Here we come up against an obvious conclusion. In many areas of economic life health efficiency is treated in an extremely primitive way. We are working towards levels of taxation on cigarettes which discourage consumption, albeit tentatively. Despite the vast amounts of damage caused by alcohol in terms of reducing fitness, traffic deaths, work loss, violence, court proceedings, family disruption, heart, liver and other diseases and addiction, there is no effective economic response in this area. There is an amazing double standard in our attitudes to health efficiency. It is foolish to require high standards within the health service while having such lax criteria in the areas of general economic life, which are still the most formative in terms of most people's life experience of health. Thus we see that the relationship between the kind of accounting used within the health service and that used in the wider economy is wildly out of kilter. The health service uses sophisticated scales, but the wider economy is scarcely into weighing lorries in terms of its sloppy responses to people's health.

Some orthodox economists reading the previous paragraph may well have been slightly puzzled. The criterion of health efficiency, although we all operate with it daily when we eat, take exercise, go to bed and have holidays, is not quite what they may have considered in terms of 'efficiency'. For often this is defined in terms of effectiveness in generating private profitability. The limitations of this criterion, however, are now painfully obvious. Manufacturers who produce cigarettes, lager and fast cars very profitably and presumably 'efficiently' in terms of production techniques, are, of course, extremely inefficient in terms of health. Their efficiency lies in producing lung cancer, liver failure and smashed faces. So we cannot assume any automatic relationship between private profitability and health efficiency and must indeed conclude that the profit-seeking private sector is sometimes drastically health-inefficient. The kind of concern with health economics and profitability which has been reflected in recent British Government approaches to reform of the health services therefore misses the point. In trying to bring in private profit-making calculations as the criteria for shaping healthcare provision, it is actually using a flawed tool. It is liable to be reaching local decisions which are silly when seen in a broader context. The problem actually lies in the closed vision adopted by this perspective which makes a virtue out of defining everything in private maximization accounting terms. To see this issue more clearly we need to review the main terms in which the medical debate has been defined for the last hundred or so years.

Applied biology, neo-classical economics, nursing and Christianity

There are a number of different perspectives which have shaped and directed the development of responses to issues of health and sickness. One of these is Christianity, which, from the earliest times, has emphasized health care, hospitals and the development of healing. All kinds of Christian initiatives were behind the international healing movement of the nineteenth century which accompanied missionary activity. Although the characterization is going to be slightly crude, I would suggest that it constitutes an important tradition with a character which is often overlooked. Part of this tradition is its emphasis on nursing, as direct personal care of the ill. The nursing tradition is also strongly associated with women, with community work, with health education and with low technology medicine. This tradition was not averse to more sophisticated developments in medical science, but was travelling in a more personal and social direction. Thus Schweitzer, towards the end of his life, working within this tradition, was quite regularly dismissed as not having kept up with developments in medical science.

A second tradition saw healthcare much more strongly in terms of the biological sciences and their application. It grew out of the emergence of the great academic disciplines as autonomous and self-referential bodies of knowledge, and was institutionally established in the links between the universities and the teaching hospitals in Britain. It developed a strong identity of professionalization based on highly developed technical expertise. In this the greatest power within the profession was held by those who appeared to have the highest level of technical competence in applied biology. This professional group has been strongly male and has gained control over nursing, midwifery, health education and community health in Britain, often through quite protracted struggles which are not fully recognized. In the Netherlands, and some other countries, this hegemony has been by no means so complete. The ideology of the group, although they would not see it as such, is that healthcare is largely a matter of applied biology, and progress occurs through pushing back the frontier of technical research. There has been a strong common commitment between medical applied biologists and the pharmaceutical industry, because drugs have been seen as a prime vehicle for implementing the applied biological vision. On the whole, this perspective has eclipsed the previous one in defining policy within the British National Health Service, although holistic medicine and other challenges have emerged more recently, and much of the personal motivation in medicine stays within the earlier tradition. It is to the economic implications of this perspective, however, that we now turn.

Within this framework the claims of biochemical research and frontier medicine know no qualification. They must be pursued. Those involved in high research have been close to funding decisions, and have shaped many of the priorities of healthcare towards high technology clinical medicine. Much of this work has been valuable, more valuable than much spent in the rest of the economy. Yet the constraints of the vision are also very important. This applied biological tunnel vision has not allowed the wider meaning of health, including its economic and social aspects, to be properly recognized. Medical care has been channelled into the hospital environment which the medical professionals control. So, for example, in Britain childbirth has been thoroughly hospitalized by doctors who effectively overrule midwifery perspectives, which see it in more personal, family and natural terms. Another effect has been a lower priority for preventative medicine over against clinical solutions. A further result has been an insistence on patients travelling to the medicine rather than medicine travelling to patients. Another has been the creation of huge biomedical empires, or hospitals, which tend to absorb all kinds of healthcare for which they are not really suited. A further effect has been the development of elaborate filtering processes, by means of which the élite professionals are protected from the public. This control and institutional tightness seem initially like strength. Actually, however, it is part of a withdrawal from a wider awareness, a withdrawal which has left the medical profession less able to respond to the wider issues of health economics and sociology, or to have any response to the question of how effective health accounting should be carried out. There was, therefore, enough evidence of medical self-indulgence in accounting to lend some weight to pressure to economize, and this tradition was sufficiently distant from members of the general public not to provide an effective opposition to the government of Mrs Thatcher.

The third ethos or tradition shaping the development of responses to health and sickness issues comes from outside the health services completely. It also reflects the emergence of self-subsistent bodies of knowledge which are reductionist. In this case it is the neo-classical tradition within economic thought. This sought to reduce all economic decision-making to a rational maximization process carried out in mathematical or accounting terms. Throughout the twentieth century this body of thought has become extremely powerful – not just academically, but in people's lives, in institutions and in the kind of political philosophy associated especially with Ronald Reagan, George Bush and Margaret Thatcher. It assumes that individuals calculate decisions about consumption on the basis of maximizing their satisfaction and that the purpose of firms is to maximize profits. It is reductionist in assuming that all values can be reduced to the single criterion of money, and that the 'real value' is the money or market value. On this view prices and market transactions become an infallible guide to the values which should prevail in a particular area. Within this perspective health becomes a commodity which people should pay for through normal market processes. The health services should therefore be run by those who are in the business of marketing health, not by the medical professionals who merely provide the services. At present there is a war between these, the applied biologists, and the market calculators, with quite a number of the younger medical staff being persuaded that they have a marketable service to provide, and opting for a neo-classical definition of the economics of health.

The problem is that the terms of the debate are severely circumscribed by the biomedical and neo-classical approaches. The biomedical approach cannot see the limitations of its own reductionist biological framework, and what is ignored in terms of the broader economic, social, psychological, ethical and educational dimensions of health. The neo-classical approach cannot see that its definition of a market for health is biased, inadequate and ignores all the broader issues of the economics of health which actually structure costs in health service provision.

1. Neo-classical health accounting

The change to seeing health as a commodity gives a fundamentally new direction to its meaning in Western cultures. First of all it moves further away from seeing health in integral personal terms. Sometimes the applied biological framework led to its own impersonal responses, people being seen as experimental, or as drug-controlled units, or as raw meat to be operated on, but the impersonal principle of the neo-classical calculus is different. It requires the construction of units of health – the provision of drugs, operations, the 'quality-adjusted life-year', doctor visits, jabs, and so on – which are marketed according to the self-governing principles of self-interested maximization. The focus of accounting is no longer the person, but the unit of health.

The underlying effect of this is to transfer authority for making decisions from those who provide the medical and other services to the accountants, who construct the cost and price constraints within which the system works. The loss of discretion is insidious. Its extent can be gauged from a similar development which occurred in British dentistry a few years back. At that time dentists were paid according to the number of fillings and extractions which they carried out. Dentists are, of course, an equally honourable profession to that of doctors, yet my mouth is one of millions which is a monument to the era when dentists were paid by the number of fillings and didn't really worry if we ate lots of sweets. The outcome was poor dental health for millions despite an unprecedented level of high quality professional activity. As the same kind of principle shapes health service provision there will be market exploitation of new forms of illness and operation, competition for units of account, and kinds of care which do not pay will be forced out of the system. Externalities which make life more difficult for patients, like travel time to more distant hospitals, queuing for services, cancelled operations, home convalescence, charges for 'privileges', loss of long-term relationships with medical staff, receiving different kinds of treatment in different places, will become more common as the internal 'efficiency' of production units is stepped up.

It is important to establish that the presumed calculation of 'efficiency' in accounting terms is bogus. There are unavoidable inequalities and noncomparabilities. An efficiently designed hospital can be 30% more efficient in energy use than a poorly designed one. Many patients are 30% less efficient in recovery than others who have serviced their bodies better, and this may be an area or regional phenomenon. Presumably some operations in the same unit category take twice as long to perform for very good clinical reasons. And most medical staff would admit that for no other reasons than experience, skill and age they have varied in efficiency throughout their careers. The accounting process also encourages a differentiation of the strong and the weak, rewarding the strong and punishing the weak. An indication of the direction of this principle is the ratio of patients to doctor: the caring model sees an equalization of this ratio as progress, but the neo-classical model sees a faster throughput of patients as progress towards efficiency. Presumably very poor countries with 30,000 or more patients per doctor are the most efficient of all. Most of this supposed increase in efficiency involves hiding costs or pushing them on to private persons or other public agencies. Sometimes this occurs through having systems of care which are less efficient in communal terms. If the accounting process was close to best medical practice, it would do least damage, but because good medical practice is flexible, open and complex, there is no possibility of this approximation occurring. Consequently, the neo-classical model can only create accounting myths which then tyrannize the practitioners.

It favours a 'McDonald's' model of fast turnover; an off-the-shelf service of health units. Within this framework various approaches can promise greater efficiency, but some of this efficiency will be perfidious. As the police might manipulate crime figures and dentists invent fillings, so doctors might invent operations. After all, these days, it is quite safe to cut people open and stitch them up again, or carry out more esoteric operations for no particular reason other than the resultant income for the unit. The structural breakdown of trust represented by the new system will be realized in patterns of deceit – medical staff cross-subsidizing areas of care which they value more than accountants do, and exaggerated claims made for the 'output' of hospitals. Most worrying of all is the pressure this model creates to see certain patients as 'inefficient' recipients of hospital care; they are better at home, or even dead. It is worth noting in passing that the administrative costs of this microaccounting are very considerable. The accountants who run the system do not reveal these costs because the extra work and responsibilities which are generated by them are never given accounting values!

One of the deepest changes with this commodity model is the movement of commitment from the person to units of output. The long process of hardening which this institutionalizes will happen imperceptibly, but surprisingly fast, through time pressures, people's work being undervalued, vicious infighting for funds, loss of trust, cuts in consulting and diagnostic care, and increasingly impersonal care. Treatment of ailments will occur in dissociation from the people who are treated. The biblical doctrine of personhood is atomized into subpersonal forms of response. It is as if the Good Samaritan left the injured person with the innkeeper with funds enough for one night's care after which he had to be ejected. Actually what the Good Samaritan said was, 'Take care of him and when I come back this way, I will pay you whatever else you spend on him.' This kind of commitment has been the mark of millions who have worked in health services. To replace it with an egocentric calculus is to replace pearls with plastic.

The model also replaces the principle of communal care with self-interested individualism. There have been four main ways of funding healthcare: individual payment, individual insurance, social insurance and national funding. In the latter two forms communal commitment is built into the process. With social insurance, the contributions of all provide a base for meeting individual needs, and national provision taps into tax and national insurance income to provide complete independence from ability to pay, and treats all citizens on the basis of need. The neo-classical model cannot cope with communal person-to-person commitments and focuses only on individual self-interested calculations. The problem with this is that often the poor and weak are most in need of healthcare yet face the highest insurance or payments costs. Meanwhile trivia that the rich can often afford to buy receive a higher priority in the markets which are supposed to give good solutions. In terms of the Good Samaritan this model insti-tutionalizes a passing by on the other side.

2. The crises in the economics of health

We thus see how deep is the crisis in the economics of health in poor countries, where the lives and health of many millions are valued so cheaply and receive so little attention. We recognize that this is not just a medical problem but reaches deep into the way the West has defined and controlled the development of the world economy. We see also the inconsistency of Western responses to health: sophistication sits alongside stampedes into gross forms of illhealth, and yet people are convinced that this absurd way of doing things makes sense. Finally, we see how Western economism is subverting the basic principles of Christian healthcare which have developed over centuries. Struggling against these trends are attempts to recapture the biblical meaning of health, and to see its economic aspect in proper focus. It is time these attempts became coherent, and significantly shaped the direction of future trends.

3. A Christian sociology of health

Again, the normal concerns in this area have focused on relationships among those who are working in healthcare and between these groups and the wider populace. There are many important issues here: male patterns of control; professionalization; issues of status, hierarchy and the use of social power; communication barriers between health professionals and the general public; the kinds of institutional life generated by healthcare; and the relationships between health workers and education, family, employers, communities, churches and media. Many Christians have come to realize that the kind of relationship which only involves imparting professional expertise to the general public is not touching the problems which patients actually bring as part of presenting as sick. Consequently they have redefined the meaning of the patient/doctor relationship in far richer social terms, thus kicking against the neo-classical perspective outlined above. These economic dimensions are important, but of far greater scope is the range of health issues which occur as part of the social lives of the general population. Health is deeply embedded in our social lives in ways which we are only now beginning to explore.

The usual perspective is one which begins from some area of disease or illness and moves back from this immediate pathology into social relationships. So, quite obviously, sexually transmitted diseases including Aids owe their existence to the patterns of social relationships which transmit them. Cervical cancer and other illnesses sometimes arise from the same source. Clearly with Aids as a pandemic there is a pragmatic attempt to modify sexual relationships in an attempt to stop its march. Sadly, this approach does not begin to get to the root of the issue, which often involves deteriorated levels of sexual relationships which go far beyond the immediate presenting problem. Thus, clearly, there are many people who in intimate relationships are prepared to put the health and lives of others at risk. There are many sexual relationships which are promiscuous and casual, involving little knowledge of or care for the partner. There are patterns of prostitution, deception of marital partners, the abuse of the young, physical abuse in sexual relationships, desertion, sexual slavery and marketing sexual partners which provide a fairly automatic context for the growth and transmission of sexual diseases, and which also generate a range of other problems. Thus, abortion usually becomes a 'solution', especially in affluent countries, when a reliable husband is not available to father the child. Its development in the West therefore largely indicates the breakdown of trust and commitment between heterosexual partners. A high proportion of excess food, alcohol, drug and tobacco consumption probably has its origin in the same area. The pragmatic approach fails to treat the relationship in its own integrity. It does not open up how central are issues of trust, commitment, love and joy to sexual relationships. It does not see how unequivocally necessary are good marriages to the health of a nation.

Another area is the transmission of addictive behaviour which damages health. Cigarette smoking is typical, usually depending on peer group initiation. Especially disturbing is the increase in cigarette smoking among women in Britain. Conformist peer pressure and image are part of this pattern, but it reflects a communal lack of personal self-respect which is serious. The same happens with alcohol consumption, drug addiction, and overeating. Again the social dynamics which produce these kinds of very important medical response are crucial and rooted in the values and attitudes transmitted from one generation to another. Often epidemiological studies, because of the categories which they choose to examine, fail to reveal the obvious: the chaste do not suffer from sexually transmitted diseases, and alcohol abuse is low among most Christian groups. Questions of personal identity, self-respect and self-acceptance are therefore basic to many of the addictive and other patterns of illness growing in Western culture. This does not mean that a pragmatic cure must be sought. The real cure, found in the message of Jesus, is simply far more comprehensive and pervasive than merely addressing these, albeit serious, problems.

All of these approaches, however, are still largely diagnostic in character and are problem orientated. What they ignore is the extent to which we depend on and help one another both in sickness and health. Much of this is familial education across generations. Much more is in patterns of dependence of the young on the old and old on the young. Some of it is help through times of weakness, illness or fatigue. There is also mutual care to avoid accidents. Diet, hygiene, rest, fitness, temperature management, cooking and drinking are also normally mutual and interdependent processes. The scope of this kind of activity exceeds the care of the organized health services many times over, yet despite its far greater importance it is normally largely ignored. Poorer countries do have educational and community programmes which aim to develop and strengthen communal healthcare, often with records of outstanding success. Yet at the same time many of the richer countries are losing these patterns of care. Young parents can no longer be taught by their parents patterns of baby and childcare, because of geographical mobility, and must learn from scratch these lessons in each generation. Mutual patterns of fitness are wiped out by car and television. Isolation and loneliness prevent patterns of mutual care which were normal a generation ago. When these social patterns of help, which are of course uncosted and not seen as part of the market economy, remain unmet and then move into the public or market sector of health, there is a sense of increased burden which is substantial and of great financial significance. This shows once again the shallowness of only taking as one's point of reference price-qualified health activities.

The overwhelming lesson which arises from consideration of all these important areas is how central love is to meeting the needs of those who are in sickness and health. It is the relationships of love in the health services and in daily life which provide the context in which people get better and renew their strength. The reason Jesus did not charge for the healings he carried out was not that he was unaware of the workings of the economy, but that direct love for the persons he met shaped his response. Health is deeply personal, both in its economic and social dimensions, and without a motivation of love similar to that of the Good Samaritan, responses finish up as empty and vain; they lose the central core of their meaning.

This is evident from another aspect of the parable of the Good Samaritan. Jesus pointedly shows the Jews that a Samaritan, a member of that despised race with whom they had few dealings, considered the healthcare of a member of their nation as important as that of his own nation. Yet the fact that the British Health Service is called the National Health Service underlines the fact that, like those of most other nations, the conception of healthcare stays fiercely nationalistic. 'If they are not one of us, they must be turned away or pay' is the general attitude. To the social question of 'Who is my neighbour?' in the provision of health services we have turned a blind eye. We have withdrawn from Jesus' invitation to follow the example of the Good Samaritan, especially in relation to the starving, sick and weak of the world. We do not even question the fact that crude tribal loyalty is the limit of our concern.

4. The full-orbed Christian response

This study is not an attack on medicine. The value and significance of medical development for healing needs to be fully honoured. It is an attack, however, on the severely limited visions associated with 'applied biology' and 'neoclassical economics'. These ideological directions, among others, have helped to create world-wide crises in health in both the poorer and richer nations. Often they are producing absurd conclusions and results, of which the most serious is the undervaluing of the health of the poor of the nations. Although this crisis has now reached acute levels, with millions dying of starvation, neither of these perspectives has begun to address it. Indeed, they seem to blind us to the possibility of doing anything: we must leave our responses to the market or to drugs.

A Christian response begins simply from the truth that personal health is God's gift, and concern for it should be reflected in our love for one another. Jesus showed this unequivocally and without reservation. It also shows us that an economics and sociology of health have an important and explicit meaning within a full-orbed understanding of health. It shows the kinds of responses which we can and do make in these areas if blessing is to follow, and also how destructive sinful economic and social patterns are for people's health. It gives us the diagnostic ability to sift the way we live and recognize how foolish and misguided our responses are. With renewed Christian hearts and lives there is no limit to the improvements which can be made to the health of the nations with God's prevenient help.

Part Two

Chapter Three

THE HOSPITAL SETTING

Michael Webb-Peploe

Consultant Physician, St Thomas's Hospital, London

Introduction

Healthcare in general, and hospital healthcare in particular, faces three major challenges.

a. The changing nature of disease

At the turn of the century, when the number of patients reaching doctors was restricted by their ability to pay, and when treatment was relatively ineffective and cheap, the doctor was able to devote time, attention, and full concentration to each individual patient. The advent of sulphonamides, and then penicillin, changed the scope of medical practice almost overnight. It shifted the emphasis from description and leisurely diagnosis with little effective treatment, to rapid diagnosis followed by appropriate therapy, which in many cases proved strikingly successful in preventing early death. As a result, the pattern of disease in the Western world has changed. Malnutrition and infection (easy to treat and 'cure') have become less common, and their place as causes of morbidity and mortality has been taken by diseases that are at least in part genetic in origin, and by degenerative disorders in an ageing population (difficult and expensive to treat, and often impossible to 'cure'). The incidence of cancer continues to rise. In part this is the natural result of increased life-expectancy, but in some cases (bronchial carcinoma and smoking, cancer of cervix and early promiscuous sex) self-indulgent habits play an important role in the causation of disease. Self-induced disease (the result of dangerous driving, of drug or alcohol overdose, of indulging in extra-marital or homosexual affairs) adds a far from negligible burden to the total healthcare load.

b. The changing pattern of hospital healthcare

In 1974, G. Bjørck[1] reported that the proportion of patients admitted to the medical beds of the Seraphimer Hospital in Stockholm as emergency cases had risen from 10% in 1958 to 70–80%. The rise was in clear contrast to the experience of the surgeons: only 30% of their ward admissions were acute cases, the rest being admitted for planned elective surgery. This rise has been the experience of every large urban hospital in an industrialized society. With limited resources, emergency medical admissions (especially in winter) too often occupy surgical beds to the detriment of patients awaiting their planned elective surgery. Bjørck identified *three* factors contributing to this change:

The first was ageing of the population, with the resultant increase of cardiovascular emergencies, coupled with a social process forcing the elderly to live alone without continuous supervision and help from members of their family. This meant that when ill, they had to find shelter and care in the hospital.

The second was an increase in the number of intoxications with sedatives, hypnotics, and other psychopharmacological drugs, often in combination with alcohol.

The third factor was failure by the primary healthcare physicians to assume effective round-the-clock responsibility for their patients. This may be because general practitioners are virtually extinct in the inner cities of Sweden and the USA, or because they have (as in many British cases) delegated all their emergency calls to a call service employing doctors who do not know the patients to whom they are called. Such doctors are sometimes ill-equipped in terms of motivation, material, and experience, and because they cannot or will not cope, take the easy way out by slapping a superficial diagnostic label on the patient, and by calling for an ambulance to transport the sufferer to the nearest hospital. 'Office hours in the modern urban society', said Bjørck, 'are 40 out of the week's 168; for the remaining 128 hours the hospitals and the police share the responsibility for the city and the citizens.'

This change in the pattern of hospital admissions has resulted in:

– displacement of less acute cases to other medical resources, particularly outpatient care;

– decreased facilities for planned in-hospital studies of patients with serious and complicated diseases, but in a non-acute phase;

– accumulation in acute beds of post-acute patients in need of care for the chronically ill, waiting for a bed in some institution for such patients, or for the organization of sufficient after-care at home (the 'blocked bed');

– forced discharge of insufficiently investigated or treated patients to make room for the acute overload;

– inability to admit to hospital patients who are seriously ill, but who can just about manage at home (though with the ever-present risk of sudden or dangerous deterioration);

– increases in the mean age of the inpatients and in the gravity of their conditions with a resulting steady increase in the demands on primary nursing care.

These trends are unlikely to be reversed in the future.

Cardiovascular emergencies cannot be prevented by preventive medicine, only postponed, and the more of them that strike older age groups, the more urgent will become the demand for hospital services, as such people too often have no family support or care.

c. Resources that are inadequate to meet ever-growing demands

As far back as 1974, Bjørck wrote:

> As far as I can see, we have passed the optimum of hospital services in the modern society, in as much as reduction of working hours with increased salaries and more demand on 'round the clock' attention to more severe cases is making the hospital the most rapidly failing enterprise of our time. There is not enough tax money to support what we already have, and at the same time there is not enough individual saving to secure private care.[2]

In facing these challenges, and in seeking to define what we mean by 'health' and 'care' we need to heed Paul's exhortation to the Romans (12:2), 'Do not conform any longer to the pattern of this world, but be transformed by the renewing of your mind. Then you will be able to test and approve what God's will is – his good, pleasing and perfect will.' It is only too easy to be led astray by contemporary thinking, much of which is confused in four key areas.

1. Confusion as to the nature of mankind – machine, animal, or human being?

The scientific study of mankind over several centuries has revealed much about the mechanical workings of man's various organs, including the 'personality-mediating' brain and central nervous system. The relatively new field of cognitive science (comprising automata theory, autonomics, communication and control theory, cybernetics, articificial intelligence) has powerfully shaped the brain scientist's thinking. It now comes as second nature to regard the brain as a means of engineering in protoplasm the kinds of information gathering and processing functions required to produce intelligently goal-directed behaviour in automata. The brain may well be *more* than that; but it is at least amenable to a great deal of detailed explanation in these mechanistic terms.[3] This has led to the view that the human being is *nothing but* a machine whose behaviour is predetermined solely by genetic and environmental factors, leaving a person no freedom of choice, and thus no responsibility for his or her actions. As with any machine, its value is judged by its utility (its contribution to 'society', to the Gross National Product). If it breaks down, you repair it; once it becomes worn out beyond repair, then it goes on the scrapheap after cannibalization for spare parts. Logic thus dictates that the old and the broken down should be marginalized in society, with the minimum of care, attention and resources devoted to them (or even actively terminated).

This rigidly mechanistic and deterministic view of humanity is not new, but a heritage from the last century, when many scientists believed that by analysing all the data of experience into the smallest possible components, one could discover the natural laws governing their movements and mutual relations. According to this view, all observed phenomena, the whole gamut of human experience, can be explained on the basis of the movement of molecules, atoms, and electrons governed by appropriate and discoverable laws. Such a cosmic view does not require the existence of God, and Laplace, when asked where God fitted into his scheme of things, replied: 'Je n'ai pas besoin de cet hypothèse'. A vaguely theistic modification of this view finds a place for God as 'prime mover', as the cosmic watchmaker who, having made the watch and wound it up, stands back and leaves the universe to tick relentlessly on its independent and predetermined course.

There is another school of thought that regards the human as *nothing but* an animal, though belonging to the most highly organized species in the animal world. This concept is relatively recent, beginning with Darwin's theories of human evolutionary origins, and receiving popular impetus over the last decade from books such as *The Naked Ape* (Desmond Morris), and in particular *Animal Liberation* (Peter Singer). In his book, Singer (Professor of Philosophy at Monash University, Melbourne) not only advocated animal rights, but essentially made no distinction between mankind and the rest of the animal kingdom with regard to the ethics of human behaviour to fellow human beings and to the animal world. In his view, 'If a being is not capable of suffering or experiencing enjoyment and happiness, there is nothing to be taken into account',[4] thus making the capacity for pleasure or pain (Bentham's utilitarian hedonic calculus) the ultimate criterion of personhood. Logically, therefore, the lives of demented or mentally defective human beings, of human infants (and especially of human foetuses) have no greater intrinsic value than those of non-human animals. These individuals, having only the same capacity for pain or pleasure as any animal, are in Singer's view 'human non-persons', and can be treated as such. The door is thus thrown wide open to unlimited foetal experimentation, and to euthanasia for humans with a non-human hedonic calculus, or those in whom the balance of pleasure versus pain has tilted too far towards pain. While most patients would not hold all of these views, many of them do regard the prime purpose of life to be enjoyment (self-gratification), so that the success or failure of healthcare is judged solely by the hedonic calculus standard of how effectively pain has been removed and pleasure restored.

In discussing the fallacy of what he calls 'nothing buttery', Donald MacKay[5] uses several helpful illustrations to point out that those who regard the human being as *nothing but* a machine, or *nothing but* an animal, are missing the vital extra dimension to human existence. The first illustration is that of flashing light signals used by ships at sea. The physicist sees them as *nothing but* light flashes that can be described so completely in terms of wavelength and periodicity that the signal can be reproduced at any time. The trained signalman, however, not only sees the light flashes, but also reads and understands the message they convey. The message is embodied in the light flashes, and adds an extra dimension to a purely physical phenomenon.

The second illustration is that of two mathematicians who 'start arguing about a problem in geometry. With a piece of chalk they make a pattern of dots and lines on the board, and the fun waxes fast and furious. Can we imagine some non-mathematician coming in, and saying in amazement, "I can't see what you are arguing about – there is nothing there but chalk?"' The idea that because in one sense, at one level, or viewed from one angle, there is nothing there but chalk, therefore it is unnecessary, it makes no sense, it is superfluous to talk about what is there in any other terms, exposes again the fallacy of *nothing buttery*. It is obvious that because the mathematicians have a different 'mind-set', a different attitude to what is there, they have the power to see in the chalk pattern an aspect and significance that the non-mathematician misses.

MacKay's third illustration is that of the computer. The electronics expert describes the computer in 'hardware' terms (components, circuit diagrams, speed of central processing chip, size of memory, and the like). This description can be so accurate as to enable the expert to construct an exact replica of the original machine. But without the program, the 'software', the computer will never fulfill its intended task, and to describe the software a different language (a programming language or machine code rather than electronic specifications and circuit diagrams) is needed. To learn the 'new language' required to understand the extra dimension to human existence that is of supreme importance, we need to turn to the Bible. In this dimension, human reason fails; what is needed is divine revelation.

The Bible tells us that the universe came into being by the act of a personal God, that he did not make the universe out of some pre-existing material, but that he created all things 'of nothing'. It also tells us that 'the Lord God formed the man from the dust of the ground' (Gn. 2:7); at the mechanical level the Bible describes humanity as dust, that is, continuous with the rest of God's physical creation. Humanity's only means of interacting with the physical environment is a body formed of the same molecules and atoms as the rest of creation, and sharing with the rest of the animal kingdom many of the same biological processes and mechanisms.

But the same verse goes on to tell us that God 'breathed into his nostrils the breath of life, and the man became a living being'; man became *nephesh*, which might best be translated as organism or mind–body. At the psychological level, man is of a piece with the animal kingdom as distinct from the inanimate world. More important, he becomes a person. This means that not only have human beings mind or consciousness, but also that the individual's mind or consciousness is a personal unity. Not merely does thinking go on within me, but it is I that think. It was I many years ago, it is the same I today, and it will be the same I to all eternity. What J. G. Machen calls 'this terrible isolation of the individual soul',[6] separated from all else in the awful loneliness of its existence as indivisible and immortal, belongs to all sorts and conditions of humanity, and is one of the things that most clearly constitutes a person. Even sin does not destroy it, though sin makes it no longer a blessing, but rather a horror and curse. It is this attribute that makes a human being, in some sense, able to communicate with God, able to be addressed by God *as a person.*

The Bible speaks of human beings being created 'in the image of God' (Gn. 1:27). God is three Persons in perfect communion in One God. Human beings are persons created to commune with God and with fellow humans. In this, they are like God. At the first, human beings were also like God not only in having personal freedom of choice, but also in that they were good. They were not created morally neutral, but their nature was positively directed to right and opposed to wrong. But though created righteous, there was still in them a possibility of becoming unrighteous. A higher state, one in which even the possibility of sinning would be removed for ever, yet remained for them to attain. Humanity was on probation, was set a test of obedience: 'you must not eat from the tree of the knowledge of good and evil' (Gn. 2:17). Obedience promised life, disobedience spelled death. If the probation had been successfully passed through, the life humanity possessed would have been assured. The 'if' would have been removed from the promise of life; the victory would have been won; nothing further could ever by any possibility have separated God from his children. But, as we know, human beings chose the way of death. They sought to attain knowledge, and lost the knowledge of good; they sought to attain power, and lost their own souls; they sought to become as God, and when God came to Adam and Eve in the garden they hid themselves in shameful fear. As MacKay points out:

> In discussion of the Genesis creation narrative, it is often insufficiently realized that the last creative act is recorded not in chapters 1 and 2, but in chapter 3. 'And God said . . . Cursed is the ground because of you . . . thorns and thistles it shall bring forth to you' (verses 17–18 RSV). In short, we are told that the created order as we know it is a *revised* version. Ours *is not the same drama* as that whose conception is narrated in chapters 1 and 2, and which God pronounced 'very good'. Some changes may for all we know have been slight; but in one far-reaching respect our natural order is radically different: for ours is a creation 'under a curse', 'groaning in travail'. Not just its human history, but the very principles of natural law reflected in the growth of weeds, the toils of life, and the inevitability of decay and death, are different from what they might have been, but for the Fall . . . The narrative of the Fall is an account of *dialogue* between man and his Creator, in which

71

man shows himself rebellious and unworthy. Moreover, in the revised version of God's created order, man is held responsible for its fallenness. Why? If Eden is for us a 'might-have-been' rather than a 'once-was', how can we be held responsible? The answer of Scripture is that 'in Adam' *we all* sinned. In some mysterious sense we *were* (or *are?* – for tenses here mislead) in Eden, at least in the sense that we have sinned Adam's sin and merited Adam's penalty. Our sin is 'original' not merely chronologically but ontologically. Here is a deep mystery, which no human analogy can parallel.[7]

The tragedy of fallen humanity, as seen by the Bible, is that having turned our backs on obedient communion with our Maker, we have lost all touch with our Creator. We are not only unfit for the relationship of a son or daughter with our Father, but we do not even want it, so far biased is our nature away from God and good, and towards evil. The result is a world of frustration and decay, of sickness and death, of relationships (not just with God and with other human beings, but also with the environment) that are tarnished and spoiled, a world of selfish attitudes and anti-social acts. Human beings are powerless to help themselves; they need rescuing. And so the key emphasis of the Bible (especially of the New Testament) is the great and mysterious rescue operation mounted by God in Christ, whereby through Christ's death on the cross, an infinitely holy God can reconcile fallen men and women (sinners such as you and I) to himself, can transform our broken and warped personalities through the power of his indwelling Holy Spirit, so that we can enter a new relationship with God, untouched even by death, In this way we are 'saved', truly made whole, granted eternal life.

So the human being is not just a body, a biological mechanism that can be explained in anatomical, physiological or biochemical terms. He or she is also an embodied soul, with a unique personality having faculties of intellect, emotion and will, capable of self-awareness and self-analysis, as well as having the ability to form relationships with others. But unless and until they are rescued by God, human beings remain (according to the Bible) 'spiritually dead'. Paul (1 Cor. 2) clearly distinguishes between the soul–man (the natural man, the embodied soul), and the Spirit–man (spiritual man), who in addition to a human soul possesses the indwelling Holy Spirit of God: 'But a soul–man (the man without the Holy Spirit) does not accept the things that come from the Spirit of God, for they are foolishness to him, and he cannot understand them, because they are spiritually discerned. The Spirit–man makes judgments about all things, but he himself is not subject to any man's judgment' (verse 14, *my translation*). This cuts right across the common notion that before a person becomes a Christian there is not much wrong with him or her except that there is one room in their being that is vacant, the room that ought to be the temple of God. Becoming a Christian (according to this view) implies merely that one part of the individual's nature, the 'spiritual' part, previously neglected, is developed and given the place it ought to have in human life. On the contrary, the Bible teaches that the real state of human nature after the Fall is not that one part of it has been amputated, or spoiled, or can attain only stunted growth, but that all of it is corrupt. The real thing that happens when someone becomes a Christian is not that God is set up and enthroned in a part of his or her nature which before was like an empty room, but that the whole person, corrupt before because of sin, is transformed by the regenerating power of the Spirit of God. (Figure 1.)

The Spirit-man and woman thus have a restored relationship with God the Father, their Creator; with God the Son, their Saviour; and with God the Holy Spirit, their Regenerator and Sanctifier. But this by no means exhausts the activities of God. He is not only Creator, but also Preserver, for as Paul expressed it to the Athenians, quoting from their own poets (Acts 17:28), 'In him we live and move and have our being'. Our continued existence and that of the whole universe and every creature in it depends

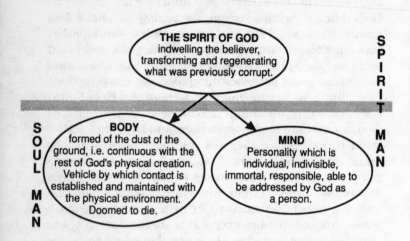

FIGURE 1. The nature of the human person.

on the preserving hand of God. Nothing created would continue to exist for the slightest fraction of a second without God. But God's activity in the universe is not limited to his keeping it from destruction. He is no cosmic watchmaker distancing himself from his creation; instead he is actively at work in it and through it in positive fashion, bringing to pass those things that are in accordance with his eternal sovereign purpose. In a secular and materialist age it is only too easy to forget that our God is omniscient, omnipotent, and omnipresent. We need constantly to remember Abraham Kuyper's words (delivered in his inaugural speech at the founding of the Free University of Amsterdam): 'There is not an inch of this universe of which Jesus Christ does not say "It is Mine".'

2. Confusion as to the definition of health

Granted the confusion as to the nature of the human person discussed in the previous section, it is not surprising that there should also be confusion as to the definition of health. Function and performance cannot be truly assessed without considering the constructional specifications, without knowing what the Designer intended. Health can be considered in terms of mental and bodily function, but this is only a fraction of the whole truth. Humans can be superb athletes, or highly intelligent, and yet be severely maladjusted with large 'unresolved personal equations'. Less physically or mentally gifted individuals are often better integrated, more mature and stable personalities than eccentric geniuses or outstanding athletes (particularly when advancing years strip athletes of their physical prowess). Physical and mental performance have to be judged in the context of age, sex, culture, social expectations and environment. Crucial to this issue is the question: 'What are people for?' MacKay has this to say:

> The Bible sets out the primary answer in uncompromising terms: men – you and I – exist to 'glorify God and to enjoy Him for ever'. The words are those of the Shorter Catechism; but the thought is solidly biblical. Human life is fulfilled in glorifying and enjoying God at three levels of relationship: 1) In our Western tradition Christians tend to think first of the *individual* relationship in which each person would ideally express his love for his Creator by constant, perfect and glad obedience and thankful communion; 2) Chronologically prior to this, and given much prominence in the Bible, is the *family* relationship. God has made people for the enjoyment of one another in family bonds of mutual expectations and love, in and through which they are also meant to enjoy fellowship with Him; 3) Finally the Bible lays great stress on the various *corporate*

relationships whereby people outside the family circle can become bound to one another by a complex of happily shared expectations and reciprocal giving, and can ideally express a corporate commitment to love and serve their God as a group or a nation.[8]

Health is thus not merely an absence of physical disease or mental disturbance, and health promotion goes far further than encouraging well-being of body and mind. Improving health in biblical terms must mean *enhancing people's capacities to relate to God as individuals and as members of family and corporate groups*. Any programme to improve the human lot that discourages the individual from dependence upon the Creator, or that destroys family bonding, or that alienates sufferers from their communities (perhaps because they feel that their care is placing intolerable financial or other burdens upon them), must be seen as short-sighted or worse:

What the Bible emphasizes, and our hearts know all too well, is the extent to which factors each desirable in themselves may interact negatively. 'Jeshurun waxed fat – and kicked' (Deuteronomy 32:15). 'It is better ... to enter into life with one eye (or hand, or foot) than having two ... to be cast into hell fire' (Mark 9:42–50). 'Not many wise men after the flesh, not many mighty ... are called' (1 Corinthians 1:26). If it was so easy for well-meaning people to make dust bowls of their environment in pursuit of desirable and legitimate ends, what dust bowls of the human spirit might not be created by analagous psychobiological developments? May not some of these indeed be with us already? When such questions as these are raised, examples come readily to mind. Health is good; but artificially stock-breeding or cloning the finest specimens of manhood at the cost of destroying the biblical ideal of family relationships would buy health at too high a cost. Self-respect is good; but a policy that gave top priority to the development of self-esteem and independence of mind, to the detriment of unselfishness and compassion, would be disastrous. Contentment is good; but the greatest unkindness we could do to a man would be to blind him to the tragedy of living with his back towards God. Contentment at that price would be an opiate indeed.[9]

In an age that venerates youth, that often regards healthcare as solely directed towards restoration of youthful vigour (mental, physical, and sexual), that sees happiness largely in terms of individual self-gratification and self-fulfilment, this emphasis that 'godliness' (salvation – a restored relationship with God in Christ) must come before 'cleanliness' (other healthcare measures) is badly needed. Paul, writing to his young friend Timothy (1 Tim. 4:8) said, 'Physical training is of some value, but godliness has value for all things, holding promise for both the present life and the life to come.' The soul–man (the person without the Spirit of God) has only declining physical strength and mental powers to look forward to with advancing years (a decline that cannot be reversed by even the best healthcare that money can buy). The Spirit–man can with Paul say (2 Cor. 4:16), 'Though outwardly we are wasting away, yet inwardly we are being renewed day by day'. (Figure 2.)

Unfortunately, in some 'demythologizing' circles today, the term 'salvation' has been degraded and means little more than 'health' – though still invested with religious overtones. The same is in danger of happening to the word 'shalom'. The result is a confusing suggestion that the gospel (God's invitation of forgiveness and restoration in Christ) and human healthcare are two alternative or even competing ways of achieving the same end. The truth is quite otherwise. One of the by-products of the restoration of our broken relationship with God should indeed be

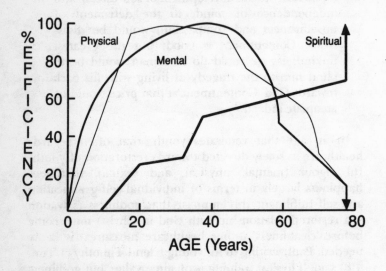

FIGURE 2. Peak physical efficiency is reached in the early twenties after which physical powers decline. Mental capacity is shown as peaking around the age of 40 (although grey cell 'fallout' starts at a much earlier age, this is compensated for by learning and experience). Spiritual growth should increase with age with full maturity reached when we depart 'to be with Christ, which is better by far' (Phil. 1:23), for then 'we shall be like him, for we shall see him as he is' (1 Jn. 3:2).

spiritual health and wholeness; but to pursue the by-product while ignoring the new relationship of which it is the fruit means forfeiting everything of lasting worth, and rejecting God's proffered salvation. By pharmacological or surgical (for example pre-frontal leucotomy) manipulations, it may be possible to turn an angry person into a peaceful one, or a suicidally depressed individual into one who is no longer a danger to himself or herself, but to a greater or lesser degree we have solved their 'personal equations' at the expense of doing violence to them as people – they have ended up with different mutilated personalities (hence our quite correct abhorrence of the treatment of political dissidents in psychiatric hospitals under certain totalitarian regimes). Only through the power of Jesus Christ as the Creator, Redeemer, and Upholder of our whole being can our personality be reshaped in a way that does no violence to us as people. Only his way of repentance, forgiveness and love preserves the continuity between us as we are now, faced with the problem of our self-centredness and rebellion against God, and us as we shall be when he has turned our hearts to God.

In Christ's view healthy people need God's salvation just as much as sick people; the physically strong and mentally agile will miss the way of eternal life without it just as completely as will the feeble and less intelligent – and may indeed be at greater risk of doing so. Human healthcare at its utopian best is no substitute for divine salvation; conversely to give top priority to salvation while ignoring or neglecting human health and the possibility of improving it runs counter to all that we learn of Christ's earthly healing ministry:

> The distinction we need to make here is between *contentment with the unalterable*, and *complacency with the alterable*, in our human condition. No doubt if our priorities were purely self-centred it could be argued that our lingering in a defective but remediable condition is our own affair; but if our primary obligation is to serve and glorify God, and if an innocuous remedy were at hand that would increase our effectiveness to that end, complacency on our part would be clearly culpable. The question then would be not: why? but: why not? If we 'daily present our bodies a living sacrifice' (Romans 12:1) it should pain us to offer our Master any needless imperfection; and whether it does or not, we rob him by doing nothing about it. In principle there is no more penetrating criterion than this one: what (with all its costs and

implications) will make the most acceptable possible offering to God? To apply this in the case of
other people, and especially of non-Christians,
may be more difficult in detail; but in essence the
criterion must be the same. 'Will a man rob God?'
(Malachi 3:8).[10]

3. Confusion as to the meaning of care

1. The confusion between care and cure

In the minds of far too many doctors, medicine is seen as
solely curative. This idea, projected by the media (who
even now are more interested in dramatic curative 'break-
throughs' than in the daily grind amd self-discipline of
preventive medicine and a healthy lifestyle) has cast the
doctor (in the eyes of the public) as the 'garage mechanic of
society' to whom you take a broken-down physical or
mental vehicle for repair, overhaul, and servicing.

Many of the current causes of morbidity and mortality
can only be palliated, and optimal treatment will demand
co-operation from patients who are fully informed about
their condition by their doctors, and prepared to make
radical alterations in their way of living.

The confusion between care and cure leads to the following consequences:

a) Doctors who, when they are unable to effect a cure say
that there is nothing more that they can do for the patient.

b) Patients who, when orthodox medicine fails to deliver
the expected rapid cure, and faced with doctors who concentrate on cure to the exclusion of care, turn to alternative
medicine (whether in the form of homeopathy, acu-
puncture, 'faith-healing' of all kinds, or the occult).

Care is not merely cure; it extends far beyond rectifying
pathology, and embraces equipping patients with the
necessary knowledge and motivation to protect and make
the most of their mental, physical and spiritual faculties so
as to live life to the full and avoid dangerous and damaging
relapses. '"Has no-one condemned you?" "No-one, sir,"

she said. "Then neither do I condemn you," Jesus declared. "Go now and leave your life of sin"' (Jn. 8:10, 11).

Cure is not care; it is sometimes part of care (but not in all cases). With the rise in genetically determined, degenerative, and self-induced disease, cure becomes more and more difficult and costly.

2. What is care?

A. *To care is to feel concern for a person, to take an interest in them*

With the ever-increasing technical content of the medical curriculum there is a danger that we are training medical technicians rather than physicians. There is the danger of losing the patient because we concentrate on all the apparatus. 'The physician has the difficult, and often impossible, task of preserving humanity in an ever more sophisticated environment. Comfort and care have to be balanced with electrodes and oxygen masks.'[11] This applies just as much to the computerized group practice as it does to the Intensive Therapy Unit. We risk looking just at the lesions, interested only in what is technically possible, neglecting to look at the patient to see what is humanely permissible.

The machine age has arrived in medicine as it has in industry:

> The most important effect of machine production
> on the imaginative picture of the world is an
> immense increase in the sense of human power
> ... There thus arises, among those who direct
> affairs or are in touch with those who do so, a new
> belief in power: first, the power of man in his
> conflicts with nature, and then the power of rulers
> as against the human beings whose beliefs and
> aspirations they seek to control by scientific pro
> paganda, especially education. The result is a
> diminution of fixity; no change seems impossible.
> Nature is raw material; so is that part of the

human race which does not effectively participate
in government. There are certain old conceptions
which represent men's belief in the limits of
human power; of these the two chief are God and
truth ... Such conceptions tend to melt away;
even if not explicitly negated, they lose importance, and are retained only superficially.[12]

These words are applicable to medicine, as they are to
society in general. Patients as 'population units', or 'trials
subjects'; patients not consulted or involved in decisions
regarding their treatment or management; patients as
syringe, catheter or scalpel fodder; audit that concentrates
solely on financial cost to the exclusion of physical and
emotional cost in the patient; the pernicious tendency to
reward managers for money saved with no account taken
of quality of care given; the widespread fraud that has
emerged in medical scientific research in recent years;
these are some of the dangers to be guarded against in the
machine age in medicine.

With the increasing technical content in modern medicine has come the need for specialization. With a high
degree of specialization, much of the technical content of
the job is repetitive, and, no matter what the skill involved,
can with the passage of time, become boring. Unless the
doctor is interested in the patient as a person (rather than
as an example of X's syndrome), he will degenerate into a
bored technician, doing a job for the money it brings in or
for the status it confers, rather than practising a caring
profession. I have met more than a few colleagues who
have lost interest in medicine and who concentrate their
thoughts and energies on other matters.

If medical students are selected purely on their academic
qualifications, and if their medical training concentrates
solely on the technical to the exclusion of the human content of medicine (and this danger is, I feel, a real one), then
we shall see a new generation of doctors who are only
interested in terms and conditions of service, in on-call
rotas, in techniques rather than in people, and whose

career choices will be dictated not by what they can give, but by what they can gain.

B. To care is to provide for the needs of someone

The needs have first to be identified. This will require a co-operative effort by both patient and doctor with ruthless honesty and self-analysis by the doctor if Illich's accusation (that the medical profession, far from being disinterested, altruistic, and enriching is rather 'dominant and disabling') is to be refuted.[13] According to Illich, doctors gain their dominance by discovering need, defining it, prescribing for it, and they alone are competent to say when need is met, that is, when patients can be discharged from their 'care'. Too often, the accusation runs, patients are maintained in a 'disabled and dependent' condition for the benefit of the professional 'carers'.

Honesty about what can, and cannot, be done; honesty about what options are available and their likely outcome; honesty about the doctor's own professional competence and that of colleagues; honesty about the contribution that the patient and the patient's family will be expected to make to his or her own care (contributions in terms of time, effort, suffering, and sometimes finance); such honesty is the only foundation on which a valid doctor–patient relationship can be erected.

Having identified the needs, they then have to be met; here the doctor is the patient's servant, willing to spend time and thought and imaginative effort and emotional energy as well as professional skill to improve the patient's condition (physical, mental and spiritual). The doctor will continue to do his or her best for the patient even if the patient refuses advice, or the prognosis is hopeless, or medically the doctor is facing defeat. The truly Christian doctor has the benefit of the indwelling Spirit of the Greatest Servant of all time and eternity. 'Whoever wants to become great among you must be your servant, and whoever wants to be first must be slave of all. For even the Son of Man did not come to be served, but to serve, and to give his life as a ransom for many' (Mk. 10:43–45). Meeting our patients' needs in these terms is costly in terms of time and effort, and may well prove to be increasingly costly in personal financial terms also as the new White Paper on the NHS is implemented.[14] It is impossible to measure the 'suffering servant' component in health care in 'cost-effective' or 'outcome' units. We cannot expect management accountants ('bean counters') and our non-Christian colleagues to be sympathetic to the view that this sort of service should be the norm. To them the cross of Christ is 'foolishness', and the exhortation to

> *Measure thy life by loss instead of gain;*
> *Not by the wine drunk, but the wine poured forth;*
> *For love's strength standeth in love's sacrifice;*
> *And whoso suffers most hath most to give*[15]

is utter nonsense.

C. To care is to hold a person in high regard, esteem, and affection

It is in this aspect of care that the Christian has a unique insight and motivation. Sydenham[16] expressed it thus: 'let him (the physician) remember that it is not any base or despicable creature of which he has undertaken the care. For the only begotten Son of God, by becoming man, recognized the value of the human race, and ennobled by His own dignity the nature He assumed.' In the incarnation, God, by stooping to become man, affirmed once and for all the value that he places on humanity, created in his image. On the cross, nailed there in our place, God expresses once and for all the lengths to which he is prepared to go, the unimaginable price he is prepared to pay to restore fallen humanity to the full glory for which he created it. Every patient, no matter how deformed the body, deranged the mind, diminished the personality, carries this double hallmark of divine value. 'Are not two sparrows sold for a penny? Yet not one of them will fall to

84

the ground apart from the will of your Father. And even the very hairs of your head are all numbered. So don't be afraid; you are worth more than many sparrows' (Mt. 10:29–31). This meaning of care is not an emotion, nor is it sentiment. It is the deliberate attitude of a mind and will submitted to a God who so loved that he gave his only Son to save a perishing world. Love for the unlovely, love for those who cannot or will not love in return thus becomes possible.

G. R. Dunstan, in a section on abortion in his book *The Artifice of Ethics*[17] contrasts two sets of values. On the one hand there are the values of care and compassion for the handicapped, values painfully acquired and handed on from generation to generation, values that owe a great deal to a Christian heritage that many are trying to deny and erode, values that bring great personal and communal rewards (the reward of gaining the trust and affection of a Down's syndrome child for example, and of helping that child achieve his full though diminished potential, the inner civilizing rewards of giving rather than getting, of service rather than selfishness). On the other hand there are the values of waste disposal, of seeking by genetic engineering to create 'the perfect specimen' (an ideal that is impossible of realization) and of throwing away the many failures.

One further thought: the cross was not the end. At his resurrection and ascension Jesus incorporated humanity into the Godhead, and seated at the right hand of God he ever lives to make intercession for us. We have all encountered patients who are 'name-droppers'. Next week they are lunching with Maggie. Jim has just rung up to find out how they are getting on. They are informing us that 'they have friends in high places so we had better treat them right or they will tell on us'. In Christ each and every one of our patients has a Friend in High Places, and One moreover who knows people so well, all of them, that he needs no evidence from others about an individual, for he himself can tell what is in a person (*cf.* Jn. 2:24–25). 'The King will reply, "I tell you the truth, whatever you did for one of the least of these brothers of mine, you did for me"' (Mt. 25:40).

I can do no better than to end this section with Trudeau's great motto: 'To cure sometimes, to relieve often, to comfort always',[18] this is care indeed.

4. Confusion as to the nature of resources

1. Material resources – money

In any discussion of healthcare resources, attention is nearly always devoted largely to money. In Enoch Powell's words, 'the unnerving discovery every Minister of Health makes at or near the outset of his term of office is that the only subject he is ever destined to discuss with the medical profession is money'.[19] It is interesting that whereas meetings on the British health service usually complain about the small percentage of the Gross National Product (GNP) spent on health, meetings in the United States have the opposite concern. On current projections, US healthcare expenditure will rise from 12% of GNP in 1989 to 14% in 1994, 18% in 2000, and (at current rates) to 100% by 2050.[20] In 1990 Americans will have spent $660 billion (roughly equivalent to Britain's total GNP) on health. And it appears that despite this massive expenditure, American healthcare is simultaneously deficient and excessive. It is deficient because about 35 million Americans (17.5% of those under 65) have no health insurance, and are dependent on charity should they fall seriously ill, and because such healthcare performance indicators as infant mortality are higher than in almost any Western European country. It is excessive because there is evidence of inappropriate and inefficient care, with only a third of carotid endarterectomies, a half of coronary artery bypass grafts, two fifths of pacemaker implantations being done on patients who are likely to benefit from these expensive procedures, and with too many hospitals performing such 'high tech' procedures as coronary bypass grafts and renal transplants in numbers too small to achieve good results at an acceptable cost per case. The thesis put forward by so many doctors that more money always means better care, is on this evidence, simply not true. There comes a point where more expenditure results in patients receiving treatment that they do not need, and that may harm them. (Figure 3.)

But it is not only a society's prosperity (or lack of it) that determines the amount it will spend on healthcare, but also its collective view of mankind, of the value to be placed on a single human life. In 1984, H. J. Aaron (an economist) and W. B. Schwartz (a physician) compared the American and British healthcare systems.[21] They concluded that while on the whole Britain compared well with the United States in dealing with life-threatening conditions (especially when these are, like cancer, dread diseases with a high degree of

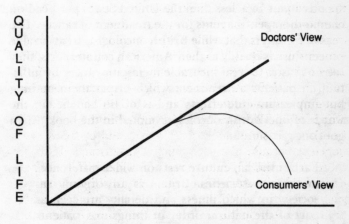

EXPENDITURE ON HEALTHCARE

FIGURE 3. For doctors more money means better care. In reality, a point is reached where more expenditure leads to poorer quality of care because people are given treatment which they do not need, and which can harm rather than benefit them. (Adapted from *British Medical Journal* 300, 1990, p. 765.)

social visibility), the NHS did relatively badly when it came to procedures designed to improve the quality of life, or to investing in equipment designed to improve diagnostic reliability. R. Klein commented that

> perhaps the most useful contribution by Aaron and Schwartz is to show that differences in the medical cultures of Britain and America are at least as important as differences in the availability of resources. The two are to an extent linked. A humane clinical conservatism in Britain both sustains and is in turn reinforced by constraints in resources. A heroic aggressive style of medicine in the United States helps to explain (and in turn to compound) the high rate of spending.[22]

One example quoted by Aaron and Schwartz is that Britain spends about 70% less than the United States per head on chemo-therapeutic agents for the treatment of cancer. The reason for this is that while British oncologists treat curable cancers just as readily as their American counterparts, they see no reason to treat incurable metastatic cancer by inflicting on patients a 'treatment which brings them nothing but unpleasant side-effects and is of no benefit', in the words of one British oncologist quoted in the book. Klein goes on:

> Each (medical) culture rests on wider differences in the two societies. Britain is an 'original sin society' in which illness and debility are seen as part of the natural order of things and patients tend to be deferential. America is a 'perfectability of man society', in which illness and debility are seen as challenges to action, and patients tend to be demanding consumers. Each culture furthermore, tends to carry its own dangers for the clinicians concerned. In Britain it is (as Aaron and Schwartz argue persuasively in the case of renal dialysis) that doctors will seek to rationalise

resources constraints (and make tragic choices more tolerable for themselves) by classifying patients as unsuitable for treatment. In the United States it is that, as Aaron and Schwartz recognise, but do not emphasize sufficiently, doctors will seek to rationalise their own desire to maximise their incomes by maximising treatment, and that activity will become an end in itself, irrespective of the outcome for the patient.[23]

Writing about health service underfunding, Geoffrey Rose has this to say:

If doctors are not primarily responsible for the nation's health then the nation is. The public, through its government, decides how much of its resources should go to the NHS. We have now realised (though only recently) that this can never be enough, and hence the miserable situation of having to decide between priorities. Dylan Thomas wrote of his father's blindness:
> *Do not go gentle into that good night*
> *Rage, rage against the dying of the light.*

We, too, should rage more than we do. We may indeed be forced to decide that there is not enough money for a woman of 65 to have a liver transplantation and the extension of life that this offers; but the fact that we must make such decisions should be accompanied by loud protest. It is society, not the medical services, who enforces these cruel options, and society (and its government) should not be allowed to turn a blind eye to what it is doing (particularly as many of these hard choices are necessary only because of such vast expenditure on armaments).[24]

In December 1973, Keith Joseph (then Minister of State for Health and Social Services) levelled this accusation at doctors:

No-one can see better than doctors the needs of
the public and the shortcomings of the NHS, but
they are not doing enough about it. I am not
aware that there has been any steady, powerful,
informed medical pressure to remedy the really
worst shortcomings. Nor am I aware that doctors
have always responded to known needs by putting their own house in order. Medical
leadership, sustained, synoptic, prepared to
agree priorities in tackling the improvements of
service to the public has not been conspicuous. It
often seems as if the NHS and the medical profession as a whole are indifferent to the miseries
they should be seeking to relieve. There has
been, and is, too little money available, but this is
no excuse for the sustained medical and lay
indifference.[25]

Such indifference springs partly from the feeling of
being a very small cog in a very large machine, with all the
important financial decisions being taken by 'faceless
gnomes' in district or regional administration. Until
recently, doctors had responsibility for patient care without power (the power of holding the purse strings),
whereas administrators had power without responsibility,
hence much of the distrust, antagonism, and 'buck-
passing' between the two groups. The recent move to
appoint clinical directors who are the budget holders for
their departments, and who, for the most part, are practising clinicians, should do something to remedy this. But
it will not increase limited financial resources, and to be
financially (as well as clinically) accountable will entail
making more (not fewer) difficult decisions with conflict
arising between compassion for the individual and for a
larger group in the population. There are two obvious
and opposite dangers: (1) Never to accept the complicated
or difficult case on the easy pretext that 'it is better for
one man to die for the people, and that the whole nation
perish not'. But in medicine, today's difficult and com-

plicated case becomes tomorrow's routine case, and if the frontiers are not explored, they never expand. (2) To treat anything and everything with inappropriate use of scarce resources, with refusal to audit outcome to see if the end justifies the means, and with the inevitable build up of cases on the waiting list that would benefit more from the available resources. To steer a correct course between these two extremes will require not only accurate cost accounting to ensure that we know what our activities (whether palliative or curative) cost, but also careful monitoring of outcome. This is to ensure that the immediate and long-term benefits to the patient (or lack of them) of any procedure are quickly established, and also that any change in procedure designed to cut costs does not do so by making the patient pay an unacceptably high price in terms of increased suffering, discomfort, inconvenience, or morbidity. An obvious example here is 'day-case' surgery. Great emphasis is currently being placed on cost accounting, but unless outcome is given equal importance, financial costs may be reduced at the expense of patients' welfare.

David Watson,[26] commenting on the stewardship of the Macedonian church described by Paul in 2 Corinthians 8 and 9, pointed out that they gave in response to God's love, in proportion to their means, in spite of hard times, in sympathy with obvious need, and as evidence of their commitment. This holds several lessons for health workers.

1. In response to God's love. If, in our daily work, we are responding to God's love, then our stewardship of medical resources will not be depersonalized, rigid, mechanical, and without sympathy, but instead caring and compassionate even when the resources to do the humanly possible are lacking. We should always comfort and relieve, even if we cannot always cure.

2. In proportion to our means. As means become more limited, so it becomes ever more important to eliminate waste. Unnecessary tests, unnecessary days spent by patients in hospital, unnecessary outpatient visits, unnecessary prescribing all have to be eliminated by humble professional introspection and an openminded willingness to change our habits in order to be able to channel resources to points of real need.

3. In spite of hard times. When morale is low, and everybody is moaning about cutbacks, and a service that has taken years of hard dedicated work to build up appears to be distintegrating, and the figures on which the funding is based are inaccurate or falsified despite all efforts to correct them, and all representations are misunderstood or ignored, it is only too easy to 'switch off', to do a bare minimum while blaming the poor service on others (administrators, politicians, greedy colleagues).

> *If you can bear to hear the truth you've spoken*
> *Twisted by knaves to make a trap for fools,*
> *Or watch the things you gave your life to, broken,*
> *And stoop and build 'em up with worn out tools:*
> *. . . You'll be a man my son.*
>
> (Rudyard Kipling)

In spite of hard times we are still called to give of our best; our best efforts to make a little go a long way, our best encouragement to disheartened colleagues, our best care and concern for the patients who are our responsibility, even if what we can do for them falls short of what is *humanly possible* through lack of funds.

4. In sympathy with obvious need. What are the obvious needs, those areas where deficiency of care most grieves God's heart of love? The hospice movement is a shining example of a Christian initiative to remedy defective care of the terminally ill. The demented (whether due to Aids, Alzheimer's disease, or other causes) present a similar challenge, as do physically or sexually abused children. We need to lift our eyes beyond our own immediate small area of concern (whether of medical specialty, of locality, or even of nationality), and be prepared to support a diversion of resources to areas of genuine need, even if it means that our slice of the cake is smaller.

5. As evidence of their commitment. Most Christians would support the concept of healthcare that is available to all according to need, regardless of ability to pay; but how much time and effort do we spend, and what sacrifices do we make in pursuit of this aim?

2. Personal resources (people)

We have to start with ourselves:

> Anyone who begins the Christian life soon observes, with surprise and dismay, the hindrance constituted by all the inner stream of dislike, complaint, criticism, anger, envy, cynicism which flows through our silent thoughts when we are doing nothing in particular, and sometimes when we are involved in activity as well. Christian holiness ... must clearly have something to do with getting rid of all this useless living and replacing it with love.[27]

More and more I am convinced that it is resentment in myself, in my colleagues, and in our patients that prevents us from making full and proper use of the enormous richness and diversity of the human resources available both in healthcare teams and in the patients they look after. Instead those resources are too often locked up in isolated strongboxes of suspicion, distrust and even hatred. It is resentment that lies at the heart of our indifference:

> The more Christian believers find their faith dealing with the problem of their resentments the more they will escape the peculiar torpor of the twentieth century. Resentment ultimately degenerates into listlessness. Genuine revolt against genuine evil, because it is not merely negative but the outcome of a positive adherence to some good which gives it energy, can fight and work without tiring. Mere resentment ultimately

sinks into a sullen inertia. There is much of this inertia in the society of our time. It is indeed the contemporary version of the sin of sloth, and it has many causes, some of which we are not yet able to identify.

Part of the cause is the standardization of life that inevitably accompanies a successful mass-production economy. The sameness of existence and the *silence about ideals* [my italics] produce a universal boredom made up of social indifference, torpid conformity, a general *taedium vitae*.[28]

By contrast:

Christians believe that human beings were made for love, for oneness with life. To approach things and people with interest and affection generally means spiritual growth. To approach them with hostility, to stand away from life and look it up and down and hit at it with some verbal weapon means decay. The personality shrivels up. The more our personalities are withdrawn and moribund, the more insignificant we feel. Then usually follow more criticism, more hostility to life, more resentment, partly because we are angry that life is so uncongenial, but also because such aggression gives the impoverished self a temporary sense of power and meaning. Much uncharitableness is the humiliated ego's attempt to feed its self-esteem by hostility.

This root of resentment can be cut only by humility, by the conviction that meaning is something that is *given* to life by God. Humility ... means that 'we are heartily content that He appoints us our place and work, and that He alone be our reward'.[29]

Resentment against another can be due to undissolved anger. The instinctive reaction to being hurt by another's words or actions is anger, the desire for revenge, the wish to retaliate in kind. If retaliation is prevented because we lack opportunity, or because we feel that revenge is morally wrong, the hot anger of the moment tends to cool and solidify into a hard lump of chronic resentment, unless dissolved by forgiveness (and what is our Christian faith about unless it is the receiving of God's forgiveness in Christ and then reflecting that forgiveness to others?).

Resentment can also be due to pride, to the feeling that others are not giving us the importance and attention that we feel is due to us:

> We shall always feel hurt if others do something that hurts our pride or fail to do something that our pride requires. It is unlikely that we shall make any progress in loving without the systematic reduction of all this unnecessary vulnerability. One of the commonest illusions of human pride is the conviction that to withhold forgiveness, to persist in resentment, is a form of asserting strength and even of effective retaliation. Actually this strategy not only maintains the pain of the injury, by keeping it in the centre of awareness, it also intensifies it, by adding to it the strain of mental conflict because we are secretly conscious of the futility, if not also the wrongness, of what we are doing. This kind of pain can only be dispelled by forgiveness. But to be able to forgive one must renounce many of the claims and illusions to which one is clinging. We cling to them for the allaying of anxiety and the production of security, but quite hopelessly because they merely increase vulnerability. It is not sufficiently understood by Christian believers how important the tragic world of pride is in the Christian theory of evil.[30]

The disappointment of extravagant expectations regarding the behaviour of others (or ourselves) can also lead to resentment:

There is a common lack of imagination and realism about human beings which must be considered part of the whole world of pretence that is foreign to love ... There is nothing people will not do under sufficient pressure and strain. It is not love but the failure of love to exempt certain people in any way from the possibility of evil. To love one's neighbour as oneself means to love him as a person like oneself, a human being whose possibilities for good and for evil are immense. The love that dare not look at life's dark potentiality is not love at all, it is fear.[31]

There is a widespread public misconception that membership of a 'caring profession' automatically confers upon the individual moral qualities of compassion and unselfishness not shared by the community at large. When the 'carer' (as too often happens) turns out to be just as selfish or greedy or ignorant or incompetent as any other professional (merely reflecting rather than transcending the community standards), disappointed (unrealistic) expectations lead to resentment, and a search for alternative 'carers'. The 'carers' too can expect too much of their patients (subservience, total compliance, gratitude, successful outcome of treatment, for example), and when these equally unrealistic expectations are disappointed, resentment is again the natural reaction. As Dunstan has pointed out:

Mutual expectation is at the heart of professional ethics ... Fidelity, in this context, means meeting the expectations appropriate to one's role. Personal integrity may often require a man to go beyond them; and always it is necessary to guard against formalism, against meeting the bare formal demand while ignoring or impairing the live, human, ethical reality of the demand behind it.

The expectations are not static: they are raised

in response to pressure from the ethical sensitivity of individuals or groups; they are lowered by insensitivity and sloth.[32]

Sensitivity, approaching people and their problems with interest and affection, humility, honesty, diligence, enthusiasm, these are some of the qualities that are required to set and meet realistic expectations of both patient and 'carer', and in so doing to improve the ethical and moral climate in the society of which we are part. For any community to survive, it must have a certain moral cohesion embodied in its conventions. As Dunstan says:

> 'Conventions' are *possible* because men are capable of moral insight, of agreeing in the recognition of moral insight, and of committing themselves to maintain it; they rest on the presupposition of fidelity to a common interest and purpose. Conventions are *necessary* because men fail conspicuously to follow their moral insights and are capable of ruthlessly exploiting one another in the pursuit of self-interest; they rest on a presupposition of infidelity to the community purpose. And in this double statement of possibility and necessity, stands the realism of ethics – and incidentally, the realism of Christian theology, which sees man as both fallen and free, turned in upon self while still ordained by nature and grace towards community and reconciliation with God.[33]

References

1 G. Bjørck, *Journal of the Royal College of Physicians* 8 (1974), p. 107.
2 *Art. cit.*, p. 107.
3 D. M. MacKay, 'Brain research and human responsibility', in M. Tinker (ed.) *The Open Mind and Other Essays* (Inter-Varsity Press, 1988), p. 69.

4 P. Singer, *Practical Ethics* (Cambridge University Press, 1979) p. 50.

5 D. M. MacKay, 'Man as a mechanism', in M. Tinker (ed.) *op. cit.*, p. 49.

6 J. G. Machen, *The Christian View of Man* (Banner of Truth Trust, 1937), p. 139.

7 D. M. MacKay, 'The sovereignty of God in the natural world', in M. Tinker (ed.) *op. cit.*, p. 189.

8 D. M. MacKay, 'Biblical perspectives on human engineering', in *ibid.*, p. 87.

9 *Ibid.*

10 *Ibid.*

11 T. F. Davies, 'The NHS is dead, long live the NHS,' *British Medical Journal* 2 (1976), p. 1376.

12 B. Russell, *History of Western Philosophy*, (Allen & Unwin, 1946; 1961 repr.) p. 699.

13 T. Illich, I. K. Zola and J. McKnight, *Disabling Professions* (Jonathan Caplan, Harley Shaiken, Marion Boyars, 1977).

14 The White Paper: *Working for Patients* (HMSO, 1989).

15 H. E. Hamilton King, 'The Sermon in the Hospital', in *The Disciples* (Kegan Paul, Trench, Trubner, 1927), p. 91.

16 T. Sydenham, *Advice to Those Entering the Profession*, ca 1670.

17 G. R. Dunstan, *The Artifice of Ethics* (SCM Press, 1974), pp. 75–88.

18 Folk saying of the fifteenth century or earlier inscribed on the statue of Dr Edward Livingston Trudeau (1848–1915) at Sarramac Lake, New York.

19 J. E. Powell, *Medicine and Politics* (Pitman Medical, 1966), p. 4.

20 R. Smith, 'Crisis in American health care', *British Medical Journal* 300 (1990), p. 765.

21 H. J. Aaron and W. B. Schwartz, *The Painful Prescription* (The Brookings Institution, 1984).

22 R. Klein, 'Rationing Health Care', *British Medical Journal* 289 (1984), p. 143.

23 *Ibid.*

24 G. Rose, 'Reflections on the changing times', *British Medical Journal* 301 (1990), p. 683.

25 Sir Keith Joseph, Marsden Lecture delivered at the Royal Free Hospital, December 1973.

26 D. Watson, *I Believe in the Church* (Hodder & Stoughton, 1978), p. 187.

27 J. Neville Ward, chapter 6, 'Resenting', in *The Use of Praying* (Epworth Press, 1967), p. 61.
28 *Ibid.*, p. 66.
29 *Ibid.*, pp. 62–63, quoting the Methodist Covenant Service, *The Book of Offices*, p. 131.
30 *Ibid.*, pp. 63–64.
31 *Ibid.*, pp. 64–65.
32 G. R. Dunstan, *The Artifice of Ethics* (SCM Press, 1974), pp. 10–11.
33 *Ibid.*, p. 7.

Chapter Four

PRIMARY CARE

Derek Munday

General Practitioner, Reading
Honorary Executive Chairman, Christians in Caring
Professions

General medical practice in this country has developed in conditions which have allowed it to become, arguably, one of the best systems of primary health care in the world. In the 1970s I remember reading a review written by a leading doctor from the USA who had been to this country in order, in his words, 'to see what lessons North American medicine could learn from medicine in Great Britain'. He was asked the question, 'What would you like to take back with you to North America?' His comment was, 'There are two things that I was greatly impressed with and would, if I had the chance, immediately institute in North America, in similar ways in which you have them here in Britain. The first one is the ward sister and the second is general practice.' Since that time the ward sister, as she was then, has been lost to National Health Service hospitals, as a result of reorganization, but general practice has continued to develop to the extent that today politicians are looking on GPs as the gatekeepers of NHS care. This, of course, has always been the case. Referral on to secondary care, in this country, has necessarily been made through general practitioners.

The rise of general practice

The acknowledgment of that role has led to the recent experiments with fund holding and the increasingly powerful status that GPs therefore have within the health-care system. Along with this experimentation has developed the understanding (many of us would say at long last), of the very important role of preventive medicine. Resources have been allocated specifically to encourage preventive medicine among GPs, *i.e.* the group of doctors in this country who are best placed, with their settled list of patients, to co-ordinate preventive health care. Money, for example, has been made available for the use of computers as a preventive medical tool, many GPs heaving a sigh of relief that at last the value of computers in that respect has been noted and resources allocated for such use.

In a national newspaper recently a survey was undertaken asking people interviewed to rate members of various professions and subgroups within those professions in order of trustworthiness and to whom they would apportion the greatest respect. General practitioners appeared at the top of the list. This is all a very far cry from the mid 1960s when general practice was in the doldrums, and could have become a diminishing and marginalized area of medical practice. The charter for general practice in those days injected life, self-respect and new vision along with the necessary resources for the development of primary care that has taken place over the last 25 years.

As we look ahead to the future it would seem that the

general practitioner will have a very important role to play in the primary care team. Increasingly primary care will become practice-based, with much of what goes on being more integrated. Secondary care in hospitals, for example, will need to take considerably more note of the general practitioner and his or her concerns and requests. In other words, it would appear that the GP may well become a much more powerful influence in the provision of health-care in this country than he or she has been to date.

Along with this political and administrative move to develop general practice has grown an interest in treating not just people's physical conditions, but also treating them as whole persons. There has been a worrying growth of a range of holistic approaches which have as their basis the use of alternative medicines, whose roots are in Eastern mysticism and philosophies. They embody a great deal of New Age teaching, and even practices that stray into the occult. A few Christians have become involved in these areas. In the face of human need and suffering, they have slipped from a biblical separation from such practices (*cf.* Dt. 18:9–12) to an acceptance of them, resulting from a feeling, often subconscious, that the end justifies the means. The seeming blanket extension of the patronage of the Prince of Wales has increased the acceptability of all types of alternative medicines.

In parallel with this, a philosophical and cultural change has taken place in British society with respect to the perception of health. As a generalization, men and women have come to believe that perfect health is their 'right'. An extension of this 'right' to health is that health must, therefore, be provided at any cost. This right to health has often been interpreted in an entirely individualistic and selfish way. This can perhaps be seen expressed in its worst form in the growing demand for abortion in this country, where the perceived rights of the mother come into conflict with the life of the unborn child. So often, the perceived rights of the mother (which are cloaked under the guise of health, normally emotional health) prevail, the life of the child being terminated – the strong taking precedence over the weak. This is a far cry from the biblical perspective and the ethics that would have existed in society not so many years ago. This 'right to health', of which abortion is a caricature, has led to ever-increasing demands for any avenue claiming to lead to health to be explored, including New Age and alternative medicines. The principle justifying this exploration being 'the right to health at any cost', the means becoming increasingly unimportant morally and ethically. General practice is caught up in the pressure of this philosophy.

A Christian doctor's response

What are Christian doctors to make of their role as general practitioners in this rapidly changing healthcare environment? How can they deliver, to the best of their ability, the key that would allow as many of their patients as possible to have the strength to be fully human? There are several dangers that face Christian doctors. As usual, they could be summed up as going too far to one extreme or another.

Medicine is a conservative profession and many Christians, especially those in the established churches, are within a Christian system which tends to be conservative in its outlook. Until the recent wave of new songs, for example, many hymns that were sung in church were several hundred years old and 'new' was something written fifty years ago! Indeed this is still the case within certain churches. Many will have found that when they try to change anything, there is an outcry from church members, with protests like 'but we have never done it that way' . . . 'I don't want change here' . . . and, 'Why can't we carry on as we have always done?' Inevitably this type of approach will rub off on to us however much we may try to guard against it. Quite unconsciously, therefore, we can fall into the trap of believing that the *status quo* is the best, and any change should be regarded with suspicion and caution and, if possible, resisted.

The result of this way of thinking is to let the secular

world make all the running. In addition to this, we have, unfortunately, a tradition whereby that which is Christian is often related only to the church structure, *i.e.* the organization of the local church, its structure, offices, buildings and the like. This would not appear to be a New Testament principle, where church was regarded as the gathering of Christians in a particular area. It had nothing to do with buildings because they did not exist, but was related to the body of people and to the activities among and outside that body of believers. The kingdom of heaven, and God's heart and desire for humankind, were not expressed just through the meeting of believers but through every area that they touched. The injunction was that even if you were a slave you should continue to serve well and bring something of the love of God into your work. Indeed, in all things, the principles of the kingdom of heaven were to apply rather than the standards set by the secular world around. Many of us have moved far from that New Testament principle within general practice, allowing the secular world to establish what is normal. Secular medical practice is, therefore, what we engage in, perhaps with a prayer now and again that God will bless us. Many may not have consciously said this but many have subconsciously slipped into this way of practice, giving the initiative to secular medicine, management structures, organizational techniques, rationalistic philosophy and increasingly, today, New Age thinking, reserving our Christian activity for church.

There is, conversely, the problem of going too far in the opposite direction, saying that there is no value in anything that is secular, that we need a total alternative, and that there is no way that God can work through medicine. People are then tempted to give up working as GPs, or as any other health professional for that matter, and seek to find some avenue of full-time Christian service through which they can really express God's heart to men and women in need.

Opportunities for care

Each of these approaches is lacking and leaves aside the opportunities that men and women in primary care have to honour God and reach their patients with his love, in a way that their non-Christian colleagues can never do.

It is necessary to find a new way where we may apply biblical principles to our practices just as much as we do to our churches. Here we would pray into all the decisions we make, putting God's will paramount – before financial gain, or before professional security or even professional respect – while we learn how to care for people, not only according to the principles we were taught in our vocational training, but primarily according to those of the Bible. How, for example, do we apply to our practice of medicine Jesus' statement that he only did that which he saw his Father doing (Jn. 5:19)? If Jesus needed to walk totally in the will of his Father, according to his Father's direction, who are we to say that we can avoid doing that? Surely even more than the Son of God we, as men and women, fallen and easily deceived, need to walk according to the principles and the direct guidance of our Heavenly Father. Although this is a general statement that can be applied to every Christian it is particularly important to those of us who deal with the pain, hurt and needs of others, because it is in this particular context that we see Jesus most clearly being effective as he worked according to his Father's will. For example, when the paralytic was lowered down through the roof in front of him, Jesus didn't immediately run to heal him. He heard what his Father was saying and started by pronouncing forgiveness for sins. He heard from his Father and then he acted. It is that principle that our enemy the devil would seek to stop us developing in our everyday work.

A Christian practice?

In this 'Christian' way of looking at primary care I propose that we need to ask ourselves the question, 'Am I unequally yoked with unbelievers in seeking to reach needs of patients?' A large area of confusion exists here. In hospital practice where Christians are employees of a hospital, they have no choice. They have to work within the hospital's rules and guidelines. GPs, however, are 'their own boss', being sub-contractors to the Health Service (a situation which is unlikely to change). In the primary healthcare team they can set the goals and the philosophy for the practice. A really good medical partnership can be a very effective tool for delivering healthcare, but it does demand that people work together with the same philosophy, although coming with different giftings and personalities.

Recently I was talking to a young doctor who had spent some time with a Christian evangelistic organization and was then enquiring how to get back into general practice. He had been given advice by a Christian GP friend that he should never join a Christian partnership because that was a 'holy huddle'. Rather he should seek to join a non-Christian partnership where his resolve, determination and development would constantly be tested and stretched. In our discussion I suggested that, having seen the possibilities of Christians working and praying together to reach men and women outside of God who were in pain and suffering, it was as foolish to join a non-Christian partnership as it would be to say to an evangelistic team, 'We have six people going out to evangelize a town ... What we need to do is have three non-Christians in the team and three Christians. That will keep us on our mettle.' Clearly in that scenario it would not work. Yet we need to be as radical in our thinking about being Christians in primary care. It is the secular world that says, 'You should not get together in Christian groups or "holy huddles".' It is the Bible that says, 'Do not be unequally yoked with unbelievers.' Admittedly, that quotation is commenting on marriage. Nevertheless, the commitment between partners in general practice, where they work well together, does have similarities. I would not apply this principle too rigidly, however, because, clearly, some Christians have been called to work in non-Christian groups. God is a God of infinite variety who will frequently break our rules. The sadness is, however, that many Christian GPs may never have considered a radical Christian approach to their medical practice and partnership. Others may not really have sought God's direction for their professional lives but have simply drifted into their present position.

The GP as modern-day priest

I have started this chapter by looking at the historical, organizational and philosophical aspects behind general practice and have done so purposely to provoke reaction. Looking after people who are ill and in need, often in great pain emotionally and spiritually as well as physically, is far too important a calling simply to be left to the direction and initiative of the secular world.

An article in a national newspaper recently talked about the general practitioner as being the 'priest of the age'. General practitioners reading this book will know how, in many respects, that is true. Without wanting it and certainly without deserving it, the role that would have been played by the parish priest earlier on this century has been transferred to the general practitioner. Anything up to 60% of the consultations in a general practitioner's surgery will be for things other than physical problems. In the eyes of many non-Christians the church has been discredited as an organization which can give them help. Yet people in an increasingly fragmented society, with high mobility, high rates of divorce, single parent families, notwithstanding all the self-help groups that have proliferated, still need to go and share their burden and pain with somebody whom they feel they can trust and who may be able to help them. So frequently this ends up being the GP.

In my experience it is not uncommon for the non-Christian patients to come and ask me to pray with them or to ask questions about specifically spiritual issues. Such issues, which are not the province of a medical practitioner but traditionally the province of the church, are so frequently brought to GPs by despairing people who don't know where else to go. The growth of all forms of alternative medicines – Eastern mysticism, yoga, meditation, and the like (increasingly supported by general practitioners) – is, in some instances, an illustration of non-Christian GPs recognizing the spiritual need, not knowing what to do with it, but realizing that conventional medicine has little to offer in this area. Yet they have stumbled on a foundational truth that health does not consist of simply making physical conditions better, nor even of dealing with emotional and psychiatric problems, but that there is also a need for the spiritual heart of humanity to find fulfilment and to come to life and health.

We may have felt that when we entered medical school we were going to be those who dealt simply with physical problems. We may even feel slightly 'cheated' by being thrust into the position of being 'the priests of the age'. Yet as Christians we have the enormous privilege of being in a position to help people to a place of true health, showing them where they can find the strength to be human. We shall need to take our courage in both hands and accept that this is not just a quirk of our civilization in the latter part of the twentieth century, but a God-given calling to follow Jesus in ministering to the pain and the need of the world. We cannot leave this to the institutional church alone. Many in need will not go to the church but they will come to the GP. The question, therefore, is how do you do it? How do you open to people that doorway to the understanding of health as the strength to be human?

Ministering to the whole person

To answer this question, we need I believe to go back to some fundamental principles. The first thing we need to recognize and accept is that we do not have the luxury of dealing with the physical part of the human being only. Christian general practitioners should recognize that God has placed them in a position where they need to care for the 'whole person', body, mind and spirit. Our medical training will have taught us how to deal with the body. We will largely have learned how to deal with the emotions, but we must recognize that the emotions and the body are also inextricably linked with the spirit of the human being. Our training for helping people spiritually will have come through the church and through our study of Scripture.

It should be noted that separating the human being into the three parts of body, mind (or soul) and spirit is a Greek idea. It is not biblical. The Bible always views a person as a 'whole'. In biblical terms, therefore, we cannot separate people into component parts, especially not in the all-embracing area of health.

We need to apply medicine, as we have learned it, to be able to effect a physical cure. Similarly we need to apply spiritual principles, as we have learned and understood them from Scripture, to be able to help men and women spiritually. We must also minister to the mind and the emotions. We must, however, see that these areas all flow together and affect each other. As general practitioners, caring for the whole person, we cannot be specialists in any one area to the exclusion of another.

We must, therefore, be prepared to be used to help people spiritually. We must pray that God will give us the grace, the means and the ability to hear what the Holy Spirit is telling us in the consulting room. We shall need to have the courage and the boldness to step beyond what we regard as conventional, *i.e.* the received body of medical knowledge. We also need to be prepared to move within the wisdom of the Holy Spirit, sometimes prompting us to do unconventional things, for example, praying for a patient for their healing, as well as treating them with conventional medicines. The greatest model for this is Jesus. Often referred to as the Great Physician, Jesus, however, was far from conventional in his ministry, moving according to that which the Holy Spirit said and what he knew to be in the heart of his Father (Jn. 5:19).

I am in no sense advocating preaching to captive audiences, nor appealing for a simply intellectual assent to the Christian faith. But if, for example, somebody comes into a consulting room saying that they have lost the will to live, there seems no point to life and, although they have everything they want, life itself seems meaningless, it may not simply be a symptom of depression that will respond to antidepressants. It may well be that that person needs to be pointed in the direction of God. Such an example really happened. The man in question very rapidly and joyfully became a Christian, finding in Jesus the answer to his question.

There are many times, of course, when somebody comes with things that are not so apparently spiritual. The wise Christian physician who has learned to listen to the voice of the Holy Spirit, may, however, unearth some simple thing that needs a spiritual solution – a prayer rather than a pill. As a result of that prayer the patient may come to a far greater degree of wholeness than any number of prescriptions or counselling sessions would have produced. I again stress that this is not to talk about preaching, rather, the whole concept of 'doing people good.' So often Jesus did not preach to people, but loved them and responded appropriately to them. He did them good. As a result of that many were blessed. Some followed him, some did not.

The place of counselling

An example of such 'doing good', taken from my own practice, would be the Christian counselling service that we have set up to help our patients. We began to recognize that many people in the highly pressurised area of the country in which we live needed counselling help. There are many counsellors in the area, ranging from psychiatrists, through psychologists and private counsellors, to frank alternative medicine and New Age practitioners. Looking at the whole variety of counselling agencies available, we realized that there was one clear counselling

111

approach that was not being addressed. The need was for skilled counsellors who were prepared to approach counselling from a Christian basis, *i.e.* the understanding of biblical principles, absolute ethics and the existence of God.

Over the years we have established such a counselling service, referring to it appropriate patients who have been offered that approach as an alternative to all others that existed. The majority of people referred would not have called themselves Christians. Many have been helped, not only emotionally, but also spiritually, even though they have not become Christians. God has touched their lives to 'do them good' just as Jesus did when he was on earth, without demanding that that could only happen if they became Christians. A few, having come through this counselling, have ultimately become Christians because they realized that that was the only way to true wholeness.

Many other initiatives are being taken around the country in the realm of primary care. New practices are being established every year where dedicated Christians, who also happen to be doctors, are seeking to find a way to help the whole person into real health. Some are exploring ways in which the local church can be involved in their practices, helping to care for those in need and developing the spiritual side of caring and health. This involvement of the church was once very evident in health provision in years gone by, when it was largely the province of the church.

It is necessary, however, to be Christians first and doctors second; to learn that if we ask Jesus to be Lord then he expects to be Lord, not only on Sunday but in every area of our medical practice – in the appointment of staff, in the manner that we work, in the way that we spend our money, in our willingness to lay down reputation and in our readiness to be radical and follow where he leads. As Christians, we shall never be able to help our patients to the area of full wholeness and health, unless we see our practice of medicine in this light. Much harm has been done to the kingdom of heaven by Christian doctors sheltering behind the comment that I often heard at medical school that, 'we should practise a high standard of medicine but, under no circumstances, speak to our patients about spiritual things'. Yet, if we are like Jesus, such spiritual counsel can be undertaken graciously, gently and humbly to the great blessing and benefit of the people we meet day by day. Is it not strange that doctors who believe in homeopathy, transcendental meditation, yoga and all forms of Eastern mysticism and, increasingly now New Age philosophies, have no qualms whatever about advertising their wares and offering them to their patients? Indeed, the profession quite happily accepts this and yet Christians often labour under the false belief that it is not right to talk about spiritual issues with patients. What a deception!

The demand for 'wholeness' will not go away when a patient's needs are not met by conventional medicine, especially if that area of need is a spiritual one. The emptiness remains and can only be filled by a spiritual solution. Many non-Christian GPs have seen the inadequacy of conventional medicine to meet spiritual need and, seeking a solution, from the best of motives, have turned toward alternative medicine, mysticism and New Age philosophies. These may seem to fill the vacuum for a while but in the end they prove to be inadequate, after being exposed as the counterfeits that they are. Surely Christians who in Jesus have found the true light of the world, the one in whom 'all things hold together' (Col. 1:17), should have no hesitation in helping men and women to find the wholeness that derives from God and his truth.

The challenges, therefore, before those of us who practise the very broad range of medicine that primary care entails, are to take with both hands the opportunity that God has given, to respond to the pain of the world around, to be radical, to learn to listen to what God is saying day by day through the Holy Spirit and in this way to seek to reach the whole person, body, mind and spirit. Such should be the stuff of Christian primary care.

Chapter Five

NURSING

Christine Chapman

Professor Emeritus of Nursing Education, University of Wales

The role of the nurse

Although most people believe they know what nursing is, nevertheless many find it hard to define. The *Shorter Oxford Dictionary* is not very helpful stating, among other things, that it is the 'activity of a nurse'. Even Florence Nightingale, widely accepted as the founder of modern nursing, was not happy with the word 'nursing', using it 'for want of another'. However, she went on to describe the work done by nurses as '... designed to keep people well, to help them avoid disease, and to restore them to their highest possible level of health'.[1] Note the order! Nurses were seen by her to be primarily concerned with keeping people well, not just with caring for the sick.

It is true to say that the role of the nurse may vary with culture and time, although it is a global activity. In some circumstances the nurse has been described as a 'professional mother', in other settings as the 'physician's assistant' while in some countries the functions of plumber, social worker, physiotherapist, cook, and the like need to be covered if the patient is to receive adequate care.

The problem is that the nurse's ability to function in this broad range of settings clouds the issue of what is the nurse's unique function. What does the nurse do better than anyone else?

Perhaps the most widely accepted definition of nursing today is that given by Virginia Henderson in a booklet she wrote for the International Council of Nurses in which she states:

> Nursing is primarily assisting the individual (sick or well) in the performance of those activities contributing to health, or its recovery (or to a peaceful death) that he would perform unaided if he had the necessary strength, will or knowledge. It is likewise the unique contribution of nursing to help the individual to be independent of assistance as soon as possible.[2]

This definition takes as its focus the whole person and considers all the functions that are normally carried out by a person while living as a complete human being. This accords well with the concept of 'health' as 'wholeness' linked with the biblical concept of shalom or peace. This peace is more than just the absence of conflict but involves total wholeness, well-being and integration of all aspects of human life. However, the definition also has an unusual component in that it makes the assumption that individuals, with the needed strength, will and knowledge, will behave in a way that will maximize their wholeness and well-being. Unfortunately, evidence to the contrary is all too frequent, witness the continuance of smoking, drug abuse and other unhealthy habits, even in the face of knowledge of the dangers involved. Some people appear to go out of their way to reduce their ability to be healthy and to negate their humanity. This should not surprise the Christian, since many people reject the way to ultimate health – that of a harmonious relationship with God. Our Lord wept over Jerusalem because they would not accept him (Lk. 13:34).

Another important component of the definition is the fact that nursing is seen as an 'assisting' activity, the nurse substituting himself or herself where the individual has an inability to act independently. Virginia Henderson amplifies what is involved in this activity by saying that the nurse is '... temporarily the consciousness of the unconscious, the love of life for the suicidal, the leg of the amputee, the eyes of the newly blind, a means of locomotion for the infant, knowledge and confidence for the young mother, a mouthpiece for those too weak or withdrawn to speak, and so on'.[3]

The needs that the nurse may be required to meet are those of daily living, breathing, eating, eliminating, resting, sleeping, moving, cleaning the body and keeping it warm and properly clothed. These needs are universal and exist independently of the diagnosis although they may be altered by it. While most of these activities of daily living appear simple to those able to perform them without assistance, to the dependent patient they become all-important and the way in which the nurse ensures that these needs are met will make all the difference to the patient's physical comfort and sense of well-being.

Meeting emotional and spiritual needs

Although nursing places great emphasis on meeting physical needs, however, these are not the only ones that may require the nurse's aid; emotional and spiritual needs also have to be met. While psychological needs have been recognized for many years it is only in the last decade that the majority of nurses have begun to acknowledge that patients have spiritual needs. Research by Simsen[4] demonstrated that most patients wanted to find answers to questions that were spiritual in nature. Many were concerned with the reason for and possible outcome of their illness and needed help to make sense of their experience. Some wished to talk to their own pastor, others needed an introduction to the hospital chaplain, but many hoped that the nurse would be able to answer their questions. This may create problems for nurses who have not come to terms with their own spiritual needs, and it may not always be easy for the nurse who is a committed Christian. Doctors and nurses are required to treat 'saints' and 'sinners' alike and not to sit in judgment over the patient's way of life. Nor should they be concerned with recruiting patients to any particular church or religious practice; however, they should be concerned with explaining the faith that is within them and be prepared to point the patient to the One who can meet all the patient's spiritual needs.

While it is obvious that people have common needs of daily living, the importance of them to the individual patient may vary, as may the way in which they may be met. Many nurses fall into the trap of assuming that they know what is best for the patient and that they have the only answer to the patient's problems. It is vital that, where the patient is capable of participating in decisions regarding the way care is carried out, the plan of care is made jointly between the patient, possibly the relatives, the nurse, and, where appropriate, other members of the healthcare team. Any other approach deprives the individual patient of part of his or her 'wholeness'.

In the 1970s, in order to ensure that the needs of patients were recognized, the nursing profession developed a systematic approach to care often called 'the nursing process'. The name, imported from the USA, is unfortunate as it indicates something 'special'; while in fact it was and is an attempt to teach nurses to look at each aspect of daily living and assess whether or not the individual has a deficit in meeting that activity. Where a deficit is recognized, a plan can then be drawn up to ensure that the deficit is made good. This may be done by the nurse or, in some cases, by other members of the healthcare team.

Finally, at the end of the period of care an evaluation of the nursing plan will reveal to what extent the patient's needs have been met.

The use of the nursing process has been regarded with suspicion by many doctors who have felt that it has removed from them authority over the care that the patient receives. This is unfortunate as the nurse is still responsible for administering treatment ordered by the doctor and does not question this part of the nursing role. It is, however, the unique function of the nurse to care for the patient 24 hours a day, and it is the nurse who is called upon to meet the patient's needs relating to activities of living.

An extension of this approach has been the introduction of primary nursing. In this situation each patient is allocated to a 'primary' nurse. It is this nurse's responsibility to assess the patient's needs, plan the care required (where possible in conjunction with the patient and/or the relatives) and remain accountable for that care until the patient is discharged. Naturally the nurse will not be on duty all day and night so others may be involved in giving care but, except in an emergency, they will not alter the care plan, without consulting the primary nurse.

Care and the nurse–patient relationship

How do patients and relatives feel about these aspects of care? S. M. Jourard states that 'One of the events which we believe inspires faith and hope in a patient is the conviction that some one cares about him.'[5] If this is true then the nurse-patient relationship is likely to be a vital factor in patient care, even more so if the patient can be introduced to the One who cares so much that the hairs of his or her head are numbered and not even a sparrow falls unnoticed (Lk. 12:6–7).

One of the difficulties is that, although the neophyte frequently enters nursing expressing the desire to 'care for people', this may not be the overt aim of the organization.

Emphasis on efficiency, cost-cutting exercises, and the need to 'get the work done' may mean that rewards are given for bureaucratic non-patient-orientated activities such as a tidy ward and good statistical records. Where primary nursing is not practised, nurses complain that it is impossible to get to know patients as individuals and that they are unable to develop any sort of inter-personal relationship. In fact in order to meet the demands of the organization many nurses find that their function is to get the patient to 'comform'. To quote Jourard again '. . . much of contemporary interpersonal competence seems to entail success in getting patients to conform to the roles that they are supposed to play in the social system of the hospital, so that the system will work smoothly, work will get done faster and patients will be less of a bother to care for'. So much for the idea of meeting patients' individual needs![6]

One important attribute required by a nurse endeavouring to treat the patient as an individual with idiosyncratic needs is that of empathy. While it is no longer considered a waste of time for a nurse to be seen talking to a patient many senior staff still frown upon the nurse who is apparently getting 'too involved'. So, talk tends to be superficial and the patient is jollied along instead of being allowed to express fears, anxieties and sadness.

Empathy requires the nurse to be able to 'step into the shoes' of the patient and feel what it is like to be in their condition. To ensure that reasonable judgment and task performance are achieved, however, the next stage of empathy is required; that is, the ability to withdraw, critically scrutinize the situation and then initiate appropriate action. It is this that distinguishes the empathy of the professional nurse from the sympathy expressed by the lay person. Although it may seem difficult for a young nurse with life before him or her to empathize with an elderly tramp facing death, appropriate education and a shared humanity, bound by a realization of the intrinsic worth of each individual, can enable the link to be made. It is here that the Christian nurse has an advantage, realizing the value placed upon each individual, so much so that God sent his own Son to die on the cross so that each and every individual person might be saved. This death ensures that all who are prepared to accept it may be truly human.

The nurse's professional conduct

The question as to whether or not nursing is a profession is often raised. Certainly nurses aspire to professional status and are frequently accorded it by the general public. Rather than enter into an argument as to the professional standing of nursing by ticking off attributes on a check list, it may be more beneficial to consider what is meant by professional action. According to A. Etzioni, 'the ultimate justification of a professional act is that it is to the professional's knowledge the right act'.[7] This involves the use of research-based knowledge to guide action (not easy in an environment which frequently places emphasis on tradition and what has 'always been done'), accountability for action (no hiding behind other members of the healthcare team) and an ability to recognize and resolve ethical dilemmas.

It is this latter point that causes most problems for nurses. The study of ethics may be said to have two aspects; the first is related to how a person 'should' behave and is based on the age-old debate engaged in by philosophers as to what is good, right and just; and the second aspect, which can almost be considered to be the obverse side of the same coin, is related to what people actually do, and the pressures – personal, cultural and organizational – which influence their actions. The first aspect may lead to statements which ignore the consequences; the second sees the result of action as the most important factor. In making an ethical decision both need to be considered.

J. P. Thiroux[8] established a set of principles of ethics which may be applied to any situation. They are:

The value of life,
Goodness or rightness,
Justice or fairness,

Truth-telling or honesty,
Individual freedom.

According to Thiroux it is important to consider each of these principles when deciding on action. For example, if it is agreed that *life is of supreme value*, then when is it appropriate to stop striving to maintain it, *i.e.* when is death a realistic option? This is the first principle, because without it the others are meaningless. However, Thiroux also states 'Human beings should revere life and accept death', which may help in making the decision to turn off a life-support system. Nurses are fortunate that they are not asked to make this decision as it lies in the hands of the doctor; nevertheless, they are part of the team that is caring for the patient and therefore cannot be seen to be uninvolved. It is also likely that it will be the nurse who will have to support the relatives, who may also have been involved in this difficult decision.

The question as to what is *good* has been debated by philosophers since the time of Aristotle, each era producing suggestions as to how an action may be judged as 'good' or otherwise. These suggestions range from looking at the original intent of the action to evaluating its outcome. Each approach has its drawbacks.

Aristotle[9] claimed that virtue lay in the appropriateness of an object or person for their task; thus a 'good knife' is one that is sharp and cuts cleanly, because cutting is the function of a knife. It may also be pleasant to look at or ugly, made of precious metal or be of little intrinsic worth, but if it does its job then it is 'good'. At first sight this is an attractive way of solving the problem of defining goodness, but close inspection reveals difficulties. What, for example, is the purpose of an individual, and can a person be described as 'good' because that purpose has been met? The Shorter Scottish Catechism states that 'The chief aim of man is to glorify God and to enjoy him forever'; while Benjamin Disraeli stated that 'Man ... is born to believe'. Now whether or not these statements are accepted it is obvious that there are individuals who, by reason of mental or physical handicap, age or infirmity, may not be able to fulfil them. Does this make them evil? Obviously not. So while the ability to function may be a useful way of discussing the value of a knife it is of no help when discussing the value of a person. Yet it is a variation of this approach that is often used, explicitly on some occasions, but more often implicitly, when deciding whether or how to treat patients. Nurses often find themselves caught up in this dilemma. The medical team decide on a course of action which to the nurse negates the value of human life. While it may be argued that the responsibility for that action lies with the doctors, it is frequently the nurse who has to carry it out.

Other ways of deciding on goodness and rightness involve the question of achieving the greatest happiness for the greatest number of people (Bentham and J. S. Mill; often used in the arguments about the 'quality of life' applied to both patients and to the unborn child to justify abortion); or of obeying one's conscience (Butler). But what happens when my conscience is saying something different to yours? And so on. All have their weaknesses and it is not the purpose of this chapter to discuss them in detail. As already stated, for the nurse the problem is often one of conflict of views. More discussion needs to take place between members of the healthcare team when deciding on courses of action and all need to remember the words of our Lord that there is only One who is good (Mt. 19:17).

One of the first things impressed upon the new nurse is that 'all people must be treated alike', that the judge is not to receive any better care than the dustman. In view of this there would not appear to be any problem with the need to be *just and fair*. However, there may be an apparent paradox in that the same new nurse will also be told that 'each person must be treated as an individual'. What is meant is that the nurse must not differentiate between individuals on the grounds of colour, class, education, attractiveness of personality, creed and so on. The only variation allowed is that required to ensure that the patient's individual needs are met. For the Christian nurse this behaviour is also a testimony to the One he or she follows. In Mark 12:14 the Pharisees, trying to trap Jesus, gave witness to his character: 'Teacher, we know you are a man of integrity. You aren't swayed by men, because you pay no attention to who they are.' This would seem easy to follow, yet in today's climate problems arise in the allocation of scarce resources and often the nurse is forced into action that may cut across the principles of justice and fairness.

This potential conflict between what may be just for the individual and what may be desired by society is not new, and finds its roots in some of the issues already discussed – the contribution or potential contribution that the individual makes to society, the happiness of the greatest number and so on. The advent of Jesus heralded a dramatic change in the way individuals were viewed. He showed concern for women and children as well as men, for slaves as well as their masters, emphasizing that to love God was to love our neighbour as ourselves. John Stott, discussing the Christian's approach to the issue of human rights, concludes: '... we have to accept that other people's rights are our responsibility. We are our brother's keeper, because God has put us in the same human family and so made us related to and responsible for one another ... we have to take more seriously Christ's intention that the Christian community should set an example to other communities.'[10] The Christian nurse shares that task.

R. Schrock[11] claims that nurses are often less than honest in their dealings with patients, yet *truthfulness* and *honesty* make up Thiroux's fourth principle. Unfortunately, while most people in present-day society would support truth-telling, an equal number would also support the use of the so called 'white lie' on the basis that to use it in some circumstances is kind. Can this ever be justified? I think not. The nurse is frequently involved, directly or indirectly, in the use of the 'white lie'. One of the biggest areas of conflict and complaint between patients, nurses and doctors is: What information should be given to the patient? Not only may some patients be told deliberate untruths when asking questions about treatment and prognosis, others are told only half the truth, and evasion is common. While appreciating that often the aim is kind the outcome of such action is almost always disaster, resulting in a lack of trust in the healthcare team. Again it is often the nurse who is asked the direct question and who, because of orders given by superiors, feels unable to give the direct reply. Many patients have a need to exert some form of control over their treatment and care and this is necessary to both their psychological and in many cases their spiritual good. Knowledge is part of this control and should be available.

Another aspect of honesty relates to the use of equipment and time and both are easily misappropriated. Yet this activity is rarely given its real name – 'stealing'. The Christian nurse has to be particularly on guard not to fall into this trap when the common practice may be such that it appears to be normal behaviour.

Finally, there is the principle of individual *freedom*. This will influence all the previously mentioned principles. It implies autonomy of action. This may apply to the patient as well as to the nurse. The nurses' Code of Professional Conduct[12] holds the registered nurse to be accountable for his or her actions. Yet, as already discussed, because the nurse may work in a team situation, decisions regarding some aspects of patient care may not be directly under the nurse's control. Accountability for these decisions rests with the person making them. However, the nurse often has to act as the patient's advocate when the patient has not the knowledge, will or strength to speak on their own behalf. The intrinsic worth of the individual must not be lost in all the other considerations relating to cost, efficiency, fees, and the like. The Christian believes that men and women are created in the image of God and must therefore be cared for with reverence. This accords well with the United Kingdom Central Council Code of Conduct, the purpose of which is laid out in its opening paragraph: 'Each registered nurse, midwife and health visitor shall act, at all times, in such a manner as to justify public trust and confidence, to uphold and enhance the good standing of the profession, to serve the interests of society and *above all* to safeguard the interests of individual patients and clients.' (Author's emphasis.)

'Wholeness' or 'shalom' is just as much a need for the nurse as for the patient. Without it the nurse may be compared to the biblical parable of the blind leading the blind. Without the wholeness that comes from reconciliation with God, the nurse will not only find it almost impossible to help to ensure that the patient's spiritual needs are met, but will be left without a sure basis from which to answer many of life's questions. These questions are fundamental to much of nursing and daily require solution.

References

1 F. Nightingale, *Notes on Nursing* (1859; repr. Duckworth, 1970), p. 6.
2 V. Henderson, *Basic Principles of Nursing Care* (International Council of Nurses, 1966), p. 3.
3 *Ibid.*, p. 4.
4 B. Simsen, 'Assessing and meeting patients' spiritual needs' (Unpublished MN thesis, University of Manchester, 1987).
5 S. M. Jourard, *The Transparent Self* (Van Nostrand, [2]1971), p. 206.
6 S. M. Jourard, *The Transparent Self* (Van Nostrand, 1964), p. 183.
7 A. Etzioni (ed.), *The Semi-professions and their Organisation* (Free Press, 1969), Preface, p. 10.
8 J. P. Thiroux, *Ethics, Theory and Practice* (Glencoe, [2]1980).
9 Aristotle, *Nichomachean Ethics*, trans. D. P. Chase (Dent, 1925).
10 J. R. W. Stott, *Issues Facing Christians Today* (Marshalls, 1984), pp. 150–151.
11 R. Schrock, 'A Question of Honesty in Nursing Practice', *Journal of Advanced Nursing* 5.2 (1980), pp. 135–148.
12 *Code of Professional Conduct* (United Kingdom Central Council for Nursing, Midwifery, and Health Visiting, 1984).

Part Three

Part Three

Chapter Six

THE CHRISTIAN AND THE PUBLIC HEALTH

Huw Francis

Formerly Area Medical Officer,
Camden and Islington AHA (T)

In a global context public health is the most protean of
concepts. From the Arctic to the Tropics, the problems
addressed in its name vary widely. The societal institutions
engaged in its pursuit – laws, departmental organization
and personnel – differ from country to country, and in any
one country from time to time. The range of tasks which
public health specialists undertake are very dissimilar:
some will be concerned solely with the control of infectious
disease, while in other countries their duties will include
the management of hospitals and the practice of forensic
medicine. The names given to this activity have been
numerous: sanitary science, hygiene, social medicine, community medicine, preventive medicine and state medicine
are but examples. The term 'public health' has no intrinsic

merit that should place it before others, except that it is at once the most traditional and the most widely used and understood.

The term has been used in the United Kingdom in four loosely connected ways.[1] Most broadly, it has meant the state of health of a defined community, national or local, and includes all that may influence it for good or ill. The traditional title and contents of the annual reports of the Chief Medical Officers of England, *Of the State of the Public Health*, illustrate the breadth of this meaning. Second, it has been used as a synonym for research into and the practice of preventive medicine. Most frequently in British usage, however, it has identified the departments and services provided by central and local government for the prevention, care and aftercare of illness. Finally, there was the minor but important use in the phrase 'public health law', denoting the laws, regulations and court rulings within which public health could be practised.[2]

Diversity is not anarchy. Wherever and whenever public health is practised, it has a strong unifying theme of the prevention of illness and the promotion of health. While it has absorbed what has been relevant in the advances in clinical medicine and the basic medical sciences, it always has as foundation to its own practice the elucidation of the health problems of the community, through population statistics, epidemiology and a pragmatic social science. The application of this knowledge and expertise has required everything from those triumphs of Victorian civil engineering – urban systems of water supply and sewerage – to teaching schoolgirls the elements of healthy childcare; from huge collective schemes for whole communities to what is individual and intimate.

'Health for All'

Present thinking about health is dominated by the World Health Organization Declaration of Alma-Ata of 1978. Member countries of WHO committed themselves to achieving health for all by the year 2000, through improved primary care. Primary care means essential care for illness and appropriate preventive measures. (Secondary and tertiary care comprise the hospital and specialist services.) 'Health for All', as the programme is called, seems at first sight foolishly utopian, but its content belies this; it is modest and practical. In the European Region of WHO, thirty-eight targets have been selected for achievement by the end of this millennium. In England some of these targets have been achieved already. Infant mortality here in 1989 was 8.4 deaths per 1000 live births; the Regional target is 20 per 1000 by the year 2000. Countries in Europe are asked to eliminate indigenous cases of poliomyelitis and diphtheria. In 1989, England had no indigenous case of poliomyelitis and only one of diphtheria. Nonetheless, highly desirable as some objectives are, they are unduly optimistic:

> By 1995, in all member states, there should be significant decreases in health-damaging behaviour, such as the use of alcohol and pharmaceutical products; use of illicit drugs, and dangerous chemical substances; dangerous driving and violent social behaviour.

That takes too little account of the Old Adam. Other desirable targets are rather vague.[3]

Detached scepticism is always wise in relation to WHO. Officers of the Organization are well aware that between a proposal and its fulfilment fall large shadows. Many member states may either be over-optimistic in reporting their progress, or some governments, while continuing to neglect the interests of their people, may cynically misrepresent their intentions. Like the unjust judge, they may yield to the importunity of the world community and be shamed into action.[4] Advances are being made, even in some poor countries of the Third World.[5] Those of us who live in the affluent countries of the West must appreciate that many developing countries, and some in the former

Eastern bloc, have economies too weak to sustain strong health sectors. But suffering is still suffering, death and grief are still death and grief even though the lines may fall in pleasant places: they level both prosperous and poor. Few have been as privileged as the princes of the nineteenth-century Anglican Church. Archbishop Tait, when Dean of Carlisle in 1856, lost within six weeks five of his six daughters, aged from eighteen months to six years, from scarlet fever. Profound sorrow is expressed in his diary:

> When I last wrote I had six daughters on earth; now I have one, an infant. O God, Thou hast dealt very mysteriously with us. We have been passing through deep waters . . . Thou hast reclaimed the lent jewels . . . [6]

With this in mind, some current public health problems will be examined.

Some contemporary public health problems

1. Environment

The WHO 'Health for All' programme stresses, as would be expected, the importance of the environment for health. The problems of general environment pollution are considered elsewhere.[7] But as well as the external environment, there are the domestic and emotional environments, hearth and home as well as locale. Where houses do not have air-conditioning, the quality of air indoors depends on that of the outside atmosphere. Internal heating appliances, however, may adversely affect the health of a household. Recently, a distant, elderly relative whose behaviour became more than usually eccentric and unpredictable, was diagnosed as suffering from early senile dementia. His symptoms disappeared completely when a defective gas water-heater was removed. Other countries have much more serious problems of carbon monoxide poisoning. In Korea the

'Ondol' system, where coal briquettes are burnt directly beneath the floor on which people sleep, causes thousands of cases of carbon monoxide poisoning each year, and hundreds of deaths. In North China, the main risk factor for lung cancer in women is not tobacco, but indoor smog caused by coal burning and poor ventilation.[8]

The European 'Health for All' targets stress that all member states should have specific programmes 'which enhance the role of the family ... in developing and supporting healthy lifestyles'.[9] The healthy emotional development of children depends on their growing up in loving, caring families. In Great Britain,[10] there has been a very steady increase in one-parent families from 8% of all families in 1971 to 16% in 1988. The circumstances of one-parent families tend to be disadvantageous when compared to families where there are two parents, either married or cohabiting.[11] Care is needed in interpreting these statistics. Many lone parents show much love and prudence in bringing up their children, making a good fist of adversity. Conversely, there are many distressed, loveless children in stable families, and some of these are in the families of committed Christians. The proportion of single-parent families is an indicator, but not a direct measure, of the problems of family life. Jürgen Moltmann draws attention to the emotional environment in which children are brought up: we have a duty to ensure their humane life (*Menschen-Lebens*), that they are 'accepted and affirmed, recognised and loved'.[12] Do not these words capture the tenderness of Jesus to children: '... whoever welcomes a little child like this in my name welcomes me ...'?[13] The toll of adult unhappiness and of mental illness, severe anxiety and depression, is very high in Western society. Its roots in childhood must concern us greatly.

2. Aids

Attention to the sexually transmitted diseases has been increased by the worldwide epidemic of Aids. Serious though the Aids epidemic threatens to be, in England at present it is far outstripped in prevalence by the other sexually transmitted diseases. Taking the most recent figures available at the time of writing, in 1989 there were 1,754 people reported to be HIV positive, but in 1988, 560,159 people attended clinics for the other sexually transmitted diseases.[14] The public education campaign in the United Kingdom has concentrated on Aids to the exclusion of the other sexual infections, and has recommended 'safe sex', that is, the use of barrier methods of prophylaxis, almost exclusively the condom. This has been deeply offensive to the Roman Catholic Church because of the contraceptive aspects, but a much wider range of Christian opinion has found the campaign's unspoken acceptance of widespread sexual relations outside marriage disturbing.[15] This assumption, it is felt, condones and encourages promiscuity.

The issue was stated most urbanely by Archbishop William Temple in an address given as President of the Central Council for Health Education, an ancestor of today's Health Education Authority. He was protesting in 1942 against a wartime regulation on the compulsory treatment of venereal disease (the former name of the sexually transmitted diseases):

> Far more potent than any teaching, any exhortation, any attempted compulsion is the suggestion afforded by habits of practice and conversation and by the attitude adopted by authority. It really is time that this elementary psychological principle should be universally accepted and acted upon: if teaching and suggestion are in conflict, suggestion will win every time. Therefore the first question we have to ask about any proposed action in this field is 'What suggestion is it offering?'

The Archbishop was in courteous conflict with another deeply committed Christian, Ernest Brown, a leading Baptist layman, and Minister of Health in Churchill's government.[16] Another who took a line similar to Ernest Brown's was Field Marshal Viscount Montgomery. Monty, as the commander of the 3rd Infantry Division in France in 1939, was concerned about the effects of venereal disease on the fighting efficiency of his troops. His divisional order on the subject was expressed with brisk, soldierly bluntness. The army chaplains were deeply shocked. In spite of his acknowledged Christian loyalties and ascetic lifestyle, he was almost dismissed.[17]

This is an issue on which men and women, with real devotion to Jesus and who observe the strictest moral standards in their personal lives, will take diametrically opposed views. Some Christians consider that, however high the cost in suffering and unhappiness, the standard of continence before marriage and fidelity within it must be maintained. Others of equal faith, contemplating the personal and social costs of the sexually transmitted diseases, take the more pragmatic views of Ernest Brown and Montgomery. The huge figure of 500,000 attending clinics, a proportion being the innocent victims of the irresponsibility of others, should make us reflect that, if anything can be done to reduce the suffering involved, it should not be dismissed lightly.

The choice between the strict and the pragmatic Christian views is not a choice between right and wrong. It is a calculation of which is the lesser of two evils: on the one hand to be strict and to accept the suffering, or to seek to limit the suffering and to appear to condone profligate behaviour. The present health education campaign with its simple message of 'safe sex' should not satisfy any Christian conscience, however, even if its necessity is accepted. It is clearly wrong not to emphasize also the overriding necessity of continence and fidelity. All continuing human relationships, if they are to be fruitful, require a basis of trust and faithfulness. One expects the milkman to deliver milk that is fresh, and not to over-charge; when one is ill, one anticipates that the doctor, within the limits of his or her knowledge and skill, will advise and treat ethically. In marriage, where part of its function is creation of a family, is there not a *prima facie* case for thinking, apart from traditional morality, that the trust and faithfulness between husband and wife should also include sexual fidelity?

Yet the contrary view is too frequently expressed. We should be aware of the influence 'the children of the permissive 1960s', now in positions of power, are having in the media and in policy making.[18] The costs of permissiveness are high. Sexual hedonism has its casualties and suffering, not least in the divorces which stem from infidelity. Is it not pertinent to ask how far the present 'safe sex' campaign is consistent with the WHO European 'Health for All' target of enhancing '... the role of the family ... in developing and supporting healthy lifestyles'?

3. Lifestyle

Lifestyle, the way we conduct ourselves from day to day, is an important contribution to our health and illnesses. A large group of disorders are now referred to as Western diseases. They include coronary heart disease, gallstones, diverticular disease of the intestine, diabetes in older people, obesity, and some cancers like those of the breast, colon, rectum and lung. These afflictions are not characteristic of pre-industrial societies. There are therefore factors in the Western environment and lifestyle which predispose to their high prevalence in Western countries.[19] Almost everyone is aware that our diet and sedentary mode of living are disadvantageous. Exercise and healthy eating are recognized as necessities for health. Yet our experience of fighting specific risk factors like tobacco does not suggest that the message of a healthy lifestyle will be accepted easily or universally; the spirit may be willing, but the body weak.[20]

The largest single cause of illness and premature death in England is cigarette smoking. Its association with lung cancer, chronic bronchitis and heart disease is well established,[21] and this grim list far from exhausts its toll. There has been a slow decline in the number of smokers, from 46% of the total population of Great Britain in 1972 to

32% in 1988. This fall has not been uniform throughout the population: only 16% of professional men smoked in 1988, compared with 43% of the unskilled. There is a similar occupational social class difference in women. What is worrying is that those who continue to smoke, smoke more heavily than before. For example, women in their fifties smoked on average 87 cigarettes each week in 1977; this had risen to a weekly average of 102 by 1988.[22] This represents a considerable reservoir of disease and suffering which will affect the community for decades to come. The prevention of cigarette smoking is complex and difficult. It is a deeply entrenched social habit. Taxation policy and the curtailing of advertising will certainly help, but the financial and political clout of the tobacco companies is considerable, not only in the West but especially in the Third World. It is a universal problem.

4. Degradation and deprivation

The discussion has focused so far principally on the problems of advanced Western countries. The degradation and deprivation of millions of people in the Third World is unspeakable. Sir Donald Acheson, then Chief Medical Officer for England, in a lecture commemorating Sir Edwin Chadwick, the great pioneer of English public health on the hundredth anniversary of his death, spoke with greater passion than is customary in the English civil service:

> Three quarters of the cities containing more than 5 million people are in developing countries. In these cities there are an estimated 100 million homeless adults and perhaps as many as 80 million homeless and in many cases abandoned children. 25% of the people in these cities have no safe water and 40% lack access to sanitation. About 30% of solid waste lies uncovered in the streets. Children brought up in these circumstances have about 40 times the mortality of other children. In

many cities in the developing world air pollution
is a much graver problem than it is in Western
cities. Prostitution, of both sexes and by no means
excluding children, is rife . . .

Many homeless people are not recognised as
official residents and their births and deaths are
therefore ignored in official records . . . [which]
helps us to ignore the problem. In these cities,
modern diseases unknown to Chadwick co-exist
with diarrhoea, malnutrition, and tuberculosis.
Smoking is being shamelessly promoted by an
industry which knows full well the lethal implications of its policies . . .[23]

Apart from the reference to smoking and modern illnesses, that could stand as description of the towns and
cities of England at the beginning of the nineteenth century.[24] The United Kingdom was the first country to pass
through the great triumphs and even greater suffering of
the Industrial Revolution, that yoking of technological
innovation and its unregulated commercial development.
One of the effects of the industrialization was a rise in
population of the towns and cities, mainly from immigra-
tion both from rural areas and from Ireland into Great
Britain. We should have no Arcadian illusions of the civic
conditions the nineteenth inherited from the eighteenth
century. The eighteenth-century towns had no sanitary
system. The houses of the poor were 'ramshackle warrens
of filth, squalor and disease . . . Disease was rampant and
unchecked: smallpox, typhus, typhoid and dysentery made
death commonplace.'[25] The Industrial Revolution multiplied and extended these horrors. It is impossible to
understand the burning zeal for public health reform of
pioneers, and the truculent tenacity of Edwin Chadwick,
unless one first grasps the stomach-turning facts of the
extreme degradation and destitution of a sizable part of
the working population.[26]
A humanitarian concern for the plight of this sub-
merged section of society was shared by all the reformers,

but all had other motives also. The first short-lived General Board of Health had four members: Lord Morpeth (later the Seventh Earl of Carlisle), a government minister, as chairman; Edwin (later Sir) Edwin Chadwick; Dr Thomas Southwood Smith; and Lord Ashley (later the Seventh Earl of Shaftesbury).[27] Chadwick, rightly honoured as the greatest English public health reformer, had fought pertinaciously for over ten years to get the Public Health Act, 1848, under which the General Board of Health was created, on to the Statute Book. As well as a humanitarian, he was an almost fanatical follower of the Utilitarian philosopher, Jeremy Bentham.[28] Shaftesbury, by contrast, had a clear Christian motivation for engaging in public health or sanitary reform. When asked by Lord Morpeth to become a member of the first Board he wrote that he had always attached 'immense and unparalleled value . . . to the sanitary question, as secondary only to the religious and in some respects inseparable from it', and '. . . I shall humbly and heartily pray to Almighty God that it may please Him, for the sake of our Blessed Redeemer to prosper His work to the glory of His own name, and the permanent wellfare (of) our beloved country.'[29]

The history of the early public health movement can be read as how we learned to live healthily in large urban communities, which were one of the legacies of the Industrial Revolution. At the spiritual level, as Shaftesbury knew, it was a confrontation with evil. It was a struggle to raise to their full stature as human beings those men, women and children whose lives had been made indescribably wretched and brutish by untrammelled exploitation by those who were 'senseless, faithless, loveless, pitiless'.[30] The same 'lordless powers',[31] that neither acknowledge God as Lord nor fellow men and women as neighbours, operate in the great cities of the Third World to keep people destitute, ignorant and nameless. They operate in Western countries so that the blessings of freedom and prosperity turn into the curse of illness and premature death. The challenge to Christians is profound.

Suffering and health

Earlier in this book,[32] David Atkinson has derived our
definition of health from the thinking of Jürgen Moltmann
and Karl Barth. Moltmann defines health both by what it is
not and by what it is. It is not a *state* as defined by WHO:
'Health is a state of complete physical, mental and social
well-being, not merely the absence of sickness and disabilities.'[33] It is an *attitude* which allows us to cope, without
loss of our humanity, with sickness, ageing and awaiting
death in peace. Health is the strength to deal with the
unavoidable vicissitudes and limitations of life; it is the
strength to be human.[34] Moltmann therefore rejects the
definition which underlies the Declaration of Alma-Ata,
and the 'Health for All' programme which at present
dominates public health practice.

There have been many criticisms of the WHO definition,
perhaps the most cogent, at the philosophical level, being
that it is so wide as to be vacuous. Nonetheless, the rhe-
torical force of the definition has to be acknowledged.
Everyone knows people who are not ill or disabled, but
neither are they fit. Furthermore there are villages and
families in Africa which have been saved from famine, and
their infectious diseases brought under control, but since
their future depends on subsistence farming in a pre-
carious climate in no sense can they be said to have social
well-being. The definition points towards the full flour-
ishing of the human spirit. Moltmann is correct to say it
sets out an unattainable ideal. Yet every physician knows
that many people in childhood and early adult life
approximate to the physical ideal and have well-adjusted
personalities. 'You are perfectly fit for your new post', is a
phrase doctors very frequently say to successful applicants
for jobs – and almost everyone at some point in their career
has been happy to hear.

Theologically, too, the ideal cannot be wished away.
John Calvin in many places expresses awe and wonder at
the human body:

> ... in regard to the structure of the human body
> one must have the greatest keenness to weigh with
> Galen's skill its articulation, symmetry, beauty and
> use. But yet, as all acknowledge, the human body
> shows itself to be a composition so ingenious that
> its Artificer is rightly judged a wonder-worker.[35]

The thrust of the thinking of Barth and Moltmann is in a different direction. Barth is very critical of a regard for health that becomes idolatry: '... they raise such things as air, sun and water ... to the level of beneficent demons to which they offer a devotion and credulity'.[36]

Health, however, is a gift from God, which must be 'affirmed and willed' both by striving to be healthy and to recover when ill.[37] Moltmann fears that if health is taken as a supreme value, it may lead to the suppression of illness and that 'the sick are pushed out of the life of society'. An individual who becomes seriously ill may lose his or her sense of their own worth.[38]

Behind Moltmann's thinking on the nature of health is his profound consideration of the relationship of suffering to the Christian faith. With remarkable courage he seeks to face the implications of the infamy of the Third Reich:

> ... I went through the remains of the concentra-
> tion camps at Maidanek in Poland. With each step
> it became physically more difficult to go further
> and look at the thousands of children's shoes,
> clothing remains, collected hair and gold teeth. At
> that moment from shame I would have preferred
> to be swallowed up by the earth ...[39]

How, he asks, is either faith in God or in being human possible after Auschwitz? 'A theology after Auschwitz would be impossible ... were not God himself in Auschwitz, suffering with the martyred and the murdered. Every other answer would be blasphemy.'[40] In the Cross, God has made all human suffering his own:

> In Jesus Christ, God himself became man ... It
> was not merely the finite and mortal aspect of
> humanity that the eternal God accepted and made
> part of his life; it was also handicapped, sick,
> weak, helpless humanity and people unfitted for
> living ... This is how God heals all sicknesses and
> all griefs, by making every sickness and every
> grief his own suffering and his own grieving.[41]

The biblical basis for this insight is Isaiah 53, particularly
verses 4 and 5, which Moltmann here translates: 'Surely he
has borne our sicknesses and carried our sorrows ...
through his wounds we are healed.'

Two things follow from this. First, Christians should
offer others a solidarity in suffering. He makes the very
penetrating observation that many who are initially willing
to help will drift away when they find that the problem
cannot be alleviated, the grief assuaged. Christian commitment 'demands a fellowship in impotence, in helplessness
and even in silence'.[42] This goes beyond the Cross to the
resurrection. One of the marks of the true church is that it
'witnesses to the glory of the risen Christ in its fellowship
with those who suffer'.[43]

Second, the death and resurrection of Christ mean that
men and women must become free from the 'vicious circles
of death' – the hopeless economic, social and political patterns that drive life towards death. One such vicious circle
is that of poverty, which consists of hunger, illness and
early mortality[44] – the traditional concerns of public
health. There is little in what Jürgen Moltmann has said to
us as Christians at the end of the twentieth century, that
John Calvin did not say in his own terms to those of the
sixteenth: that rulers should have due regard to the
Second Table of the Law and give justice to the poor;[45]
that the church should use its means to relieve the needy;[46]
and, expounding the Sixth Commandment, 'Thou shalt
not kill', that it is the duty of each of us: '... if we do not
wish to violate the image of God, we ought to hold our
neighbour sacred. And if we do not wish to renounce all

humanity, we ought to cherish his as our own flesh . . .'[47]

Public health has little difficulty in adapting to the view that the definition of health should begin with considering suffering rather than the ideal – or does it? The main way in which public health specialists explore the health status and problems of the community is by mortality and morbidity rates. William Farr, appointed in 1839 as the first medical statistician to the General Registry Office (now the Office of Population Censuses and Surveys) said:

> How the people of England live is one of the most
> important questions that can be considered; and
> how – of what causes, and at what ages – they die
> is scarcely of less account; for it is the complement
> of the primary question teaching men how to live
> a longer, healthier and happier life.[48]

How he used this insight can be illustrated by his analysis of violent deaths in the quinquennium 1852–6. In England in those five years, 7,739 persons died of burns. In those cases where the cause was known, 2,239 died from their clothes catching fire and 1,642 of these were children aged 10 or younger. 'The discovery of these appalling facts', said Farr, 'will, it may be hoped, lead to new precautions against this danger.' With prescience which anticipated events by a hundred years, he predicted that clothes might be made incombustible chemically.[49]

In this essay the problems which have been discussed have been identified by illness or by premature death: carbon monoxide poisoning, emotionally disturbed children, Aids and other sexually transmitted diseases, and the major diseases – lung cancer, chronic bronchitis and heart disease – related to cigarette smoking. The facts about mortality and morbidity are relatively easy to collect in the Western democracies; there are very considerable difficulties, as Sir Donald Acheson pointed out, in the Third World.[50] Surveys of health and fitness are possible, but they are much more difficult to undertake.

To measure health in terms of mortality and morbidity

does not necessarily imply sympathy with those who suffer. It is an extreme example, but an instructive one: Bernard Häring, the Roman Catholic moral theologian, relates how in the Third Reich, the nursing Orders were asked how many children for whom they cared in hospitals and homes had hereditary diseases. Many nuns hid such children, saying they had none. The real question was not how many are there, but how many handicapped children are there for us to take and eliminate.[51] There are, however, some people concerned with the prevention of illness and the promotion of health, who do so from a rejection of the sick, the aged and the handicapped. They may otherwise be people of a humane spirit, but their concern for health is not in itself healthy. More generally, mortality and morbidity rates do not directly measure suffering, though obviously they are related to it. If an elderly, homeless man with no known relatives dies friendless and alone, while it may strike those who deal with him as a tragedy, sadly his death will effect no-one deeply. If the same man had been a beloved grandfather, he will be missed by many, and the sorrow may linger. Each death will count as one in the statistics; the degree of grief each causes is very different.

The challenge of Moltmann's thought is that our concern for the health of the community should arise not from any concept of the ideal, nor even from the contemplation of suffering, but from our solidarity with the suffering of known persons. One of the seminal works which influenced the early public health movement was an essay published by James Phillips Kay (later Sir James Kay-Shuttleworth) in 1832: *The Moral and Physical Condition of the Working Classes Employed in the Cotton Manufacture in Manchester*.[52] It was stimulated by the great cholera epidemic of that year. As a young physician he was called to the house of an Irish family in some of the worst slums in the city. The father was very ill. Dr Kay sat by his bed for some hours. Sir James relates 'As twilight came on the sufferer expired . . .'. The widow and her three children were taken to the emergency cholera hospital. When he went to see them about midnight, the infant had died. 'The mother was naturally full of terror and distress ... I sat with her and the nurse by the fire far into the night ...' Within the next few hours the whole family died of the disease.

This episode made a profound impression on him. He visited and investigated the first 250 cases which occurred, an important part of the evidence on which his essay was based.[53] In 1832 neither the cause nor treatment of cholera was known. Young James Phillips Kay showed to a pauper Irish family, in a slum house by the River Medlock, and in the emergency hospital (a converted cotton mill in Knot Hill) 'a fellowship in impotence, in helplessness and silence'.[54] It was from such solidarity with the suffering of the poor that the great nineteenth-century work for the downcast began. Cecil Ashley, Shaftesbury's sixth son, described the crowds lining the route of his father's funeral as 'the halt, the blind, the maimed, the poor and the naked standing bare-headed in their rags amidst a pelting rain ... to show their love ... to their departed friend ...'.[55] 'Happy', said Sir John Simon, 'the land where professed religion bears fruit in such a life as his.'[56]

The challenge of public health

In the evangelical contribution to the improvement of social welfare in the nineteenth century, William Wilberforce and Shaftesbury are but the most illustrious names among many. With this inheritance it is a matter for surprise that John Stott can speak of the 'temporarily mislaid social conscience' of the evangelical movement between 1920 and 1970.[57] Because of the need to oppose liberal theology, evangelicals tended also to regard as heterodox anyone with a social dimension to their Christian thinking. Unfortunately, that attitude has not wholly disappeared. Yet the challenge to be concerned about the poor and the needy is unmistakable in the gospels.

The pursuit of public health is irreducibly political. Primarily it has been concerned with the framing of laws and their passage through Parliament. The responsibility for the administration of that legislation has been in the hands of politicians – ministers in central government, elected councillors in democratic local government. Christians who wish to promote the public health cannot avoid the political aspects. The involvement of the church in politics is, however, much misunderstood.

The first duty of any church which wishes to have a political impact is not the making of grand public statements on burning issues, or trying to influence active politicians. It is the appropriate pastoral care of the congregation. Anyone with experience, both of the social provisions of the British State, and of evangelical churches, will be aware of two related facts. The staff of these public services have a higher proportion of people with a Christian commitment than the general population; and many evangelical churches have among their adherents a higher proportion of these public servants – nurses, health visitors, environmental health officers, social workers, teachers and doctors – than the community at large. These are responsible for carrying out agreed public policy. The more senior and gifted may contribute to shaping policy, and may, through participation in their professional bodies, influence thinking in their professions. The more influential professional bodies have direct access to government ministers and senior politicians in the opposition parties.

This diaspora of Christian influence in the structures of the world should be cherished. All professions in the public services are under stress. Those dealing personally with patients, clients or pupils often have to deal with distressing personal circumstances; those with administrative or managerial responsibilities are frequently faced with complex decisions. The difficulties discussed in the prevention of Aids and the sexually transmitted diseases illustrate this. Compassion-fatigue and 'burn out' are not uncommon. The first pastoral duty is support and encouragement. Many churches will covet for their own use the gifts and experience of these people. There is an almost forgotten Christian teaching that should be recalled. The secular employment of the lay person is itself a divine vocation, however humble that work may be.[58] The Christian's primary Christian duty is in the world, not the local church.

If we follow Moltmann's view of health, then our concern to prevent illness must arise from our solidarity with the suffering. The gathered churches of Nonconformity have no parish, and the successful evangelical Anglican churches now have many resemblances to gathered congregations. The welfare state has removed the most obvious needs. Yet in any community there are many who are suffering and lonely. Most evangelical causes will faithfully evangelize the area they serve, but how many offer an undemanding friendship to those in need, who are not already adherents? Can it really please the Lord if, in offering the Bread of Life to outsiders, we appear to be stonily indifferent to their physical plight? It is significant that in most Christian churches, severely handicapped people are present at our regular worship in numbers far less than their proportion in the community. Many of our church buildings are difficult or impossible for wheelchairs to enter. Solidarity has to be more than notional.

If Christian churches are to make a political impact, what points are important in relation to the public health? The *first* is that the sick and disabled within society at large are not marginalized. Any ideology which promotes the '*Volk*' or national fitness or efficiency risks such a rejection. The sick and the handicapped still bear the image of God. Witness to their worth is crucial. The *second* follows from it: the idolatry of health must be resisted. Health is a means to service, not an end in itself. *Third*, we must protest against both undue individualism and its opposite, the tyranny of the collective. As Christians we must be concerned with the common good. Nothing can be common unless potentially it can be expressed in all the individuals who make up that community. At the basis of any Christian concept of the common good must rest the love of our neighbours. *Fourth*, we must be concerned about justice and equity. In England there is a maldistribution of health services between North and South. There are marked and continuing differences between the health of the affluent classes and the poor. These differences pale almost into insignificance when we compare the health status and services of the wealthy Western democracies and countries of the Third World. Is not the West in these matters rather like the rich man in relation to Lazarus? The solution to these inequalities raises issues well outside the scope of this essay, like the huge burden of Third World debt, and is a matter of international politics.[59] When the discrepancies are so great, can the evangelical churches remain indifferent? With the extent of rapid worldwide transport, health, like peace, is global and indivisible; it is a matter of prudence as well as justice.

The issue of lifestyle and health should cut deep into the Christian conscience. Apart from certain specific risks, of which smoking is the prime example, the advice to be moderate in all things covers most of what is meant by lifestyle. Evangelical Christians are as prone to the Western diseases as non-Christians. In general our lifestyle does not differ so markedly from our neighbours in our consumer orientated societies. The general health of committed Christians is not noticeably better. But it goes further than this. The general lifestyle of Western democracies depends on our societies using more than our fair share of the earth's resources, to the disadvantage of poorer countries. Both from the point of view of conserving the earth's resources, and of not exploiting poorer nations, a radically simpler lifestyle is desirable.[60] Richard Foster[61] speaks of the spiritual discipline of simplicity. As a witness to a true view of personal health, to the need to conserve the good things of God's creation, and to the needs of our distant neighbours overseas, should we not consider whether a simpler lifestyle is enjoined on us?

This essay necessarily has been of the earth, earthy. It has emphasized mortality and morbidity, illness and suffering. The purpose has been to point to the reverse of these – health and happiness. Without happiness there is no true health. For the Christian the concept of health points beyond a temporal happiness to the true Christian joy and hope. There can be no better statement of the Christian motive in social welfare, including the public health services, than General William Booth's last and perhaps greatest speech:

> *While women weep as they do now, I'll fight;*
> *while little children go hungry as they do now, I'll fight;*
> *while men go to prison, in and out, in and out, I'll fight;*
> *while there remains one dark soul without the light of*
> *God, I'll fight – I'll fight to the very end.*[62]

Notes and references

1 H. Francis, 'Public health: the decline and restoration of the tradition', in M. Warren and H. Francis (eds.), *Recalling the Medical Officer of Health: Writings by Sidney Chave* (King Edward's Hospital Fund, 1987), pp. 152–153.

2 The Acheson Report (*Public Health in England*, HMSO, 1988 CM289) has recently defined public health as 'the science and art of preventing disease, prolonging life and promoting health through the organised efforts of society'. This represents a combination of the second and third uses of the term.

3 Department of Health, *On the State of the Public Health 1989* (HMSO, 1990), *passim*.

4 Lk. 18:1–6, AV.

5 E. Tarimo and A. Creese (eds.), *Achieving Health For All by the Year 2000: Midway Reports of Country Experiences* (World Health Organization, 1990).

6 R. T. Davidson and W. Benham, *Life of Archibald Campbell Tait, Archbishop of Canterbury* (MacMillan, 1891) vol. 1, pp. 189–190.

7 See below, Chapter 7.

8 Editorial, 'Indoor pollution in developing countries', *Lancet* 336 (1990), p. 1548.

9 Department of Health, *op. cit.*, p. 159.

10 The United Kingdom consists of four countries: England, Scotland, Wales and Northern Ireland. Great Britain is the largest island of the British Isles, and includes England, Scotland and Wales. When England is referred to in this essay the single country England is meant, and not any larger grouping.

11 Office of Population Censuses and Surveys, *General Household Survey 1988* (HMSO, 1990), p. 13 and tables 2.19 to 2.23.

12 J. Moltmann, *The Experiment Hope* (SCM Press, 1975), p. 166.

13 Mt. 18.5.

14 Department of Health, *op. cit.*, pp. 88–103.

15 Just how widespread is this acceptance is illustrated by a comment in *The Times* (14th January 1991, p. 27) by a woman student at Manchester University: 'When I first arrived, everybody kept throwing sex at you. One first lecture was on family planning advice, the college newspaper issued free condoms and there were advertisements everywhere about safe sex. I know we are meant to be the Aids generation, but just because we are students does not mean that sex is the only thing we think about.'

16 F. A. Iremonger, *William Temple, Archbishop of Canterbury* (Oxford University Press, 1948), pp. 449–450.

17 'My view is that if a man wants to have a woman, let him do so by all means: but he must use his common sense, and take the necessary precautions against infection – otherwise he becomes a casualty by his own neglect, and this is helping the enemy . . . We must face up to the problem, be perfectly frank about it, and do all we can to help the soldier in this very difficult matter.' Quoted by Nigel Hamilton, *Monty: the Making of a General, 1887–1942* (Hamish Hamilton, 1981), pp. 334–335.

18 A. Doran, interview with Lord Rees-Mogg, Chairman of the Broadcasting Standards Council (*Daily Mail*, 2nd January 1991).

19 N. J. Temple and D. P. Burkitt, 'The war on cancer – failure of therapy and research', *Journal of the Royal Society of Medicine* 84 (1991), pp. 95–98.

20 Mt. 26:41; Mk. 14:38.

21 Non-medical readers may not appreciate that many factors contribute to the development of these maladies in individuals; their genesis is multi-factorial. Non-smokers may, therefore, develop them. Cigarette smoking is a very powerful cause, so that the risk of smokers being affected is very much greater.

22 Office of Population Censuses and Surveys, *General Household Survey 1988* (HMSO, 1990), Department of Health, *On the State of the Public Health 1989* (HMSO, 1990), pp. 38–40.

23 E. D. Acheson, 'Edwin Chadwick and the world we live in',

150

Lancet 336 (1990), pp. 1482–1485.

24 The course of public health reform has differed in the countries of the United Kingdom. The oddities of British constitutional law lie outside the scope of this essay. With no disrespect to the Scots, the Irish and more recently my own nation, for convenience the historical references relate mainly to England.

25 J. H. Plumb, *England in the Eighteenth Century* (Penguin, 1963), pp. 12–13.

26 See G. Himmelfarb, *The Idea of Poverty* (Faber, 1984).

27 Sir John Simon, *English Sanitary Institutions* (John Murray, 1897) *passim* but especially pp. 205–206. The position of the medical member of the Board was complicated, see pp. 206 and 209–210.

28 S. E. Finer, *The Life and Times of Sir Edwin Chadwick* (Methuen, 1952; Repr. 1970), p. 513.

29 G. B. A. M. Findlayson, *The Seventh Earl of Shaftesbury* (Eyre Methuen, 1981), pp. 277–278.

30 Rom. 1:31. Professor C. K. Barrett's translation in his *The Epistle to the Romans* (A. & C. Black, 1957; 1984 repr.) p. 32.

31 K. Barth, *The Christian Life* (T. & T. Clark, 1981), pp. 213–233.

32 See above, Chapter 1, pp. 33–34.

33 J. Moltmann, *God in Creation* (SCM Press, 1985), pp. 271–272.

34 *Ibid.*, pp. 272–273.

35 John Calvin, *Institutes of the Christian Religion* I, v, 2. J. T. McNeill and F. L. Battles (eds.) (Westminster Press and SCM Press, 1960), pp. 53–54. Galen of Pergamon (AD 129–99) was a physician who, among other things, made early studies of anatomy.

36 K. Barth, *Church Dogmatics* (T. & T. Clark, 1961), III/4, p. 357.

37 *Ibid.*, pp. 356–357.

38 J. Moltmann, *God in Creation*, pp. 273–274.

39 J. Moltmann, *The Experiment Hope*, pp. 72–73.

40 *Ibid.*

41 J. Moltmann, *The Power of the Powerless* (SCM Press, 1981), p. 147.

42 *Ibid.*, p. 110.

43 J. Moltmann, *The Church in the Power of the Spirit* (SCM Press, 1977), p. 361.

44 J. Moltmann, *The Crucified God* (SCM Press, 1974), p. 330.

45 Calvin, *Institutes* IV, xx, 9 (pp. 1495–1496).

46 *Ibid.*, IV, iv, 8 (pp. 1075–1076).

47 *Ibid.*, II, viii, 40 (pp. 404–405).

48 W. Farr, *Vital Statistics* ed. by N. Humphreys (The Sanitary Institute, 1885), p. 116.

49 *Ibid.*, p. 294.

50 See E. D. Acheson, 'Edwin Chadwick and the world we live in', *Lancet* 336 (1990), pp. 1482–1485.

51 B. Häring, *Free and Faithful in Christ* (St Paul Publications, 1979), vol. 2, p. 48.

52 J. P. Kay, *The Moral and Physical Condition of the Working Classes Employed in the Cotton Manufacture in Manchester* (James Ridgway, 1832).

53 B. C. Bloomfield (ed.), *The Autobiography of Sir James Kay-Shuttleworth*, Education Libraries Bulletin, Supplement 7 (London University Institute of Education, 1964), pp. 9–11.

54 J. Moltmann, *The Church in the Power of the Spirit* (SCM Press, 1977), p. 361.

55 J. Pollock, *Shaftesbury, the Poor Man's Earl* (Lion, 1990), p. 184.

56 Sir John Simon, *English Sanitary Institutions* (John Murray, [2]1897), p. 235.

57 J. R. W. Stott, *Issues Facing Christians Today* (Marshalls, 1984), p. xi.

58 Calvin, *Institutes*, III, x, 6 (pp. 734–735); R. S. Wallace, *Calvin's Doctrine of the Christian Life* (Oliver & Boyd, 1959), p. 155.

59 See P. Vallely, *Bad Samaritans* (Hodder & Stoughton, 1990).

60 See H. Dammers, *A Christian Life Style* (Hodder & Stoughton, 1986).

61 R. Foster, *Celebration of Discipline* (Hodder & Stoughton, 1980), pp. 69–83.

62 R. Collier, *The General Next to God* (Collins, [2]1976), p. 220.

Chapter Seven

HEALTH AND THE ENVIRONMENT

R. J. Berry

Professor of Genetics, University College, London

The Ministers of the Environment and of Health in the Member States of the European Region of WHO met together for the first time in December 1989, and approved a 'European Charter on Environment and Health'. This states as the first criterion for public policy that:

> Good health and wellbeing require a clean and harmonious environment in which physical, psychological, social and aesthetic factors are all given their due importance. The environment should be regarded as a resource for improving living conditions and increasing wellbeing. The preferred approach should be to promote the principle of 'prevention is better than cure'.

It asserts that 'Every individual is entitled to an environment conducive to the highest attainable level of health and wellbeing', and that 'Every individual has a responsibility to contribute to the protection of the environment, in the interests of his or her own health and the health of others.'[1]

It is easy to be cynical about sweeping pronouncements from politicians, particularly in situations where they cannot easily be called to account, and it is fair to ask how relevant the Charter is to clinical practice. A moment's thought, however, will identify a host of 'health' (and disease) problems which result from a distortion of the relationship between the individual and his or her environment – stress, trauma, pathogen or parasite assault, poisoning, malnutrition. The list could be section headings in a pathology textbook, and such would be a proper way of dealing with them. It would also be a limited and negative way. We are all individuals, and all live in an environment which affects us in various ways, both helpfully and detrimentally.

This chapter is about the individual in context. I use the word 'context' to mean 'environment' in the widest sense – human and non-human, family and other relationships, biotic and abiotic influences. We are raw material, body-minds made in God's image. Our context is constantly and ever more rapidly changing in time and in space. The Bible describes the 'raw material' as spirit-filled dust – a body made from existing components, which God differentiated by transformation into his image. It lays down principles for understanding and exercising our environmental interactions. Every generation is called upon to work out afresh the practicalities of these principles as our knowledge enlarges. Our environmental attitudes should be different to an Old Testament patriarch or even a nineteenth-century farmer, because our context is vastly different.

Environment and health

The preamble of the European Charter begins: 'In the light of WHO's strategy for health for all in Europe [and] the report of the World Commission on Environment and Development ...'. The WHO objective is well-known to doctors; the World Commission on Environment and Development is likely to mean nothing to most people in the medical profession. It is perhaps more recognizable as the Brundtland Commission, an independent group under the chairmanship of Gro Harlem Brundtland, Prime Minister of Norway in 1981, 1986 and 1990, and formerly a practising doctor. The group was set up by the United Nations Organization in 1983 on the pattern of the Brandt Report (on economics) and the Palme Report (on disarmament).

The task of the Brundtland Commission was:
– to re-examine the critical issues of environment and development and to formulate innovative, concrete, and realistic action proposals to deal with them; and
– to strengthen international co-operation on environment and development and to assess and propose new forms of co-operation that can break out of existing patterns and influence policies and events in the direction of needed change.

The report was published in 1987 as a book, *Our Common Future*. It introduced the term 'sustainable development' to common use, a concept underlined by the then British Environment Minister, Chris Patten, as 'only through development which is sustainable can countries such as ours continue to grow. And more importantly, only in this way can less developed countries break the vicious downward spiral of poverty leading to environmental degradation, leading to greater poverty, and so on.'

In her preface to *Our Common Future*, Gro Brundtland made the important point which makes her Report relevant to health:

> The environment does not exist as a sphere separate from human actions, ambitions, and needs, and

attempts to defend it in isolation from human concerns have given the very word 'environment' a connotation of naivety in some political circles ... But the 'environment' is where we all live; and 'development' is what we all do in attempting to improve our lot within that abode. The two are inseparable.[2]

The Brundtland Report is undoubtedly one of the most important documents for the end of the twentieth century. Many of its concerns are not relevant to this book, but its emphasis on ecological interdependence is fundamental to the practice of good medicine and the attainment of 'the strength to be human'.

The individual in context

Modern drugs and anaesthesia, asepsis, and scanning technologies have revolutionized medicine. Doctors can now cure patients instead of merely treating them. But they have had a damaging consequence, in that it is now only too easy to deal with diseases rather than patients. This is a trend which has been fought by Christians, but with only limited success. After all, if we are ill, our first priority is recovery rather than an idealistic state of 'health'. The same processes, however, which have led to reductionism in medicine have led also to the possibility of analysing its problems. This is perhaps clearest in psychiatry, where the phase of believing that virtually all psychoses would succumb to the right drug is now long gone; good psychiatry involves treating the 'whole person'.

But what is the whole person? Until we have a clear idea of this, we will never be able to determine whether a disease can be treated in isolation, or whether it should be considered in the context of other influences. And at the outset we have to recognize that there is a surprising lack of agreement about the true nature of humanity. For years there has been a strong reductionistic tradition that we are no more than machines, completely describable in physicochemical language, in principle wholly predictable in physiological and behavioural terms. It is a distinguished and important tradition which is important in medicine because much organic disease can be dealt with by assuming it is true. The tradition is descended from Descartes and the great physiologists, Pavlov, Skinner, and the behaviourists, and those like Robert Ardrey, Desmond Morris, Konrad Lorenz and Edward Wilson who argue by analogy from studies on animals. It has never taken over completely, however, from the older belief that we are more than animals, and that there is a complementary side to our being which distinguishes us from all non-humans. This 'nonmechanistic' part of our nature is sometimes portrayed as a dualism, but has been justified rigorously by W. H. Thorpe, Michael Polanyi, and in particular by Donald MacKay.[3] The inadequacy of the 'machine-only' understanding has been powerfully exposed by S. A. Barnett in *Biology and Freedom*.[4]

This is not the place to set out in detail the complementary factors which constitute human nature, but a digression is necessary to outline the Christian understanding of *Homo sapiens*. Since we are concerned with the relationship of the individual with his or her environment, it is important to state the Bible teaching that we are differentiated from the animals by possessing the 'image of God'. Scripture is silent about any anatomical or physical differences, although we are 'like the beasts' (Ps. 49:12, 20). John Calvin is explicit about this. In his *Commentary* on Genesis 2:7 he wrote: 'Man is linked with the natural creation by his body being made of the same substance as the rest of creation,' but he is distinct from it because he is 'endued with a soul, whence it received vital motion; and on the soul God engraved his own image, to which immortality is annexed'. The account of the creation of humankind in Genesis 2:7 says that only when the Lord God 'breathed into his nostrils the breath of life' did the body he had formed become 'a living being'. Wholeness involves body plus spirit. The parallel account in Genesis 1:26, 27 refers to God making human beings 'in (his own) image'.

The Bible never defines the image of God, and it is unwise for us to be too precise. The concept, however, clearly refers to a correspondence or special relationship with God. Karl Barth points out that our distinctiveness is that we alone are 'faced by God, and have to make responsible decisions before him'.[5] Emil Brunner agrees, arguing that God's image is like a reflection (2 Cor. 3:18) so that 'Man's meaning and his intrinsic worth do not reside in himself but in the One who stands "over against" him in Christ, the Primal Image' (Col. 1:15).[6] C. F. D. Moule concludes: 'The most satisfying of the many interpretations of the image of God in man is that which sees it as basically responsibility (Ecclesiasticus 17: 1–14).'[7]

The significance of this digression is that a human being who is a 'God-imaged animal' (or a body-soul) may respond differently to his or her environment (in the widest sense) than a creature who is nothing but an animal (Ps. 104:20–23). Although we can deny the possession of a soul or claim that it makes no difference to our behaviour or reactions, we cannot disprove its existence.[8] And for a Christian, humanness necessarily involves God's spirit in each of us.

Variation

Although all humans are members of the same species and all are alike in being judged by God (Rom. 3:22, 23), we are each a unique individual with particular traits and talents. Even identical twins diverge as they experience different environments and accumulate somatic mutations, although they are, of course, much more like each other than any other pair of individuals. Human variation is a fact of life as well as being a complication for doctors – and often a cause of confusion. Sexual and racial variation, for example, has frequently been used to claim superior status for particular groups, usually Caucasian white males.[9] There is no justification whatsoever for this: all the evidence is that *Homo sapiens* is a highly polymorphic and polytypic unitary species, with a greater range of variation within races than between the interracial averages for any trait.

Of much more medical significance is the amount of individual variation, placing some people at risk (or protected) from particular hazards or treatments. It is generally accepted, for example, that smoking disposes towards lung cancer, but a substantial number of heavy smokers never develop lung cancers, and a smaller number of non-smokers do so. More than half a century ago, J. B. S. Haldane pointed out the implications of inherited variation towards disease in a characteristically lucid way:

> I should be interested to know whether the death rate among potters is still eight times that of the general population. If so, it would not be unreasonable if a certain proportion of the funds devoted to pottery research at Stoke-on-Trent were spent on research on potters rather than on pots. But while I am sure that our standards of industrial hygiene are shamefully low, it is important to realize that there is a side to this question which has so far been completely ignored. The majority of potters do not die of bronchitis. It is quite possible that only a fraction of potters are of a constitution which renders them liable to it. If so, we could eliminate potters' bronchitis by rejecting entrants into the pottery industry who are congenitally disposed to it ... There are two sides to most of the questions involving unfavourable environments. Not only could the environment be improved but susceptible individuals could be excluded.[10]

Such exclusion tends to be labelled 'discrimination' and not discussed. For example, sickle-cell haemoglobin, which confers inherited protection against falciparum malaria, is regarded by many blacks (among whom it mainly occurs) as a racial discriminant. To identify an HIV-infected person is claimed to be an intolerable invasion of privacy.

Sensitivity (or resistance) to particular drugs may be life-threatening. An excellent example of this is carriers of the allele for porphyria variegata, who lapse into a potentially fatal apnoea (cessation of breathing) when treated with therapeutic doses of sulphonamides.[11] The allele is generally rare, but is relatively common among South Africans of Dutch descent. Other well-known gene/drug interactions involve suxamethonium and isoniazid. Pharmacogenetics is now an established sub-discipline of pharmacology and therapeutics.[12]

Ecological genetics

Pharmacogenetics is part of the wider subject of ecological genetics, a topic which owes more to the Oxford lepidopterist E. B. Ford than anyone else (although probably not – as claimed by the American geneticist R. C. Lewontin – to 'the fascination with birds and gardens, butterflies and snails which was characteristic of the prewar upper middle class from which so many British scientists came').[13] His interest in the maintenance of variation, and the role of heterozygous advantage in determining polymorphism (originally shown by R. A. Fisher),[14] led Ford to argue that the frequencies of the human blood groups are affected by various diseases, and to search for associations between particular blood groups and diseases. Although many such associations are now known (for example, group O people are 40% more likely to get a duodenal ulcer than other people; group A people are 20% more likely to get stomach cancer than others), most of the associations are fairly weak and the diseases mainly degenerative ones of later life. The most likely explanation for blood group differentiation is that they represent differential responses to past epidemic diseases.[15] Notwithstanding, some of the regional difference in disease patterns is almost certainly due to heterogeneity in allele distribution.

The 'raw material' of ecological genetics is biogeography, or in the medical context, the geography of disease. Ford's own work built on the description by natural historians of local races and particularly forms of butterflies and moths; the medical counterpart is the mapping of different diseases.[16] The next stage is correlating incidence (or frequency) with possibly relevant environmental factors (such as coronary heart disease and water hardness). Burkitt's studies of diet and the 'diseases of civilization' are classical here.[17] (Other examples are leukaemia and background geology, and smoking and lung cancer; the examples are many.) Finally, a causal link has to be established between environmental agent and condition; this is the most difficult part of the study. Sometimes this can be done by experiment (as with A. C. Allison's demonstration[18] of the difference between sickle-cell carriers and non-carriers when exposed to malarial infection) or by clinical trial. Sometimes it is only possible to test inferences when people at risk migrate or change their behaviour (or diet).[19]

Two empirical discoveries have transformed ecological genetics. The first was the recognition that strong selection pressures are common, at least in non-human populations. The second was the finding that inherited variation is far more common in virtually all species than was previously assumed. The latter derived from the application of the well-established biochemical technique of protein electrophoresis to population samples. The first two reports appeared in 1966 from H. Harris[20] (working on humans in London) and R. C. Lewontin and J. L. Hubby[21] (working on fruit flies in Chicago); since then several thousand species have been scored with the conclusion that around 5–15% of gene loci scored were heterozygous, *i.e.* different alleles inherited from the two parents.

This is not the place to review the debates of the 1970s and 1980s between selectionists and neutralists. Suffice it to say that the classical neo-Darwinian theory has been largely confirmed,[22] albeit with a clearer emphasis on ecological and non-deterministic processes than when population genetics was in the thrall of theoreticians.[23] The important conclusion for the purpose of this chapter is that the genetic constitution of an organism is the consequence of processes of adaptation through generations, and is not a random collection of irrelevant variation. Species have been moulded by their environments. It is improper to seek understanding of our life and reactions in isolation from our environment – and this caveat applies to the human species as much as other species.

Holism and reductionism

Returning from ecological genetics to variation in general: the feature which distinguishes biology (and medicine is applied biology in this discussion) from virtually all other sciences is the existence of variation. Darwin's insight was really nothing more than the recognition that variation adds a radical new dimension to the struggle for existence. Carl Pantin has emphasized the same point – variation underlies all biology. It is not merely an inconvenient complication. He wrote:

> *Physics and chemistry have been able to become exact and mature just because so much of the wealth of natural phenomena is excluded from their study* [Pantin's italics]. There is no need for the physicist as such to go to biology for data until in the last resort he has to take into account that the biologist is a living creature. I would call such sciences 'restricted'. In contrast, biology and geology are 'unrestricted'. Men of science devoted to these fields must be prepared to follow the analysis of their problems into every other kind of science.[24]

This holistic view of the world is vehemently rejected by some as leading to woolly thinking and retarding the advance of scientific understanding. There are two answers to this. Firstly, good science (never mind effective medicine) must take into account all the relevant data, and not merely the convenient ones. We need to distinguish between the operational reductionism necessary for scientific experiment and clinical diagnosis, and operational reductionism which assumes that any system can be accounted for wholly by the properties of its components and which consequently ignores both emergent properties and variation.[25] Secondly, we must beware of assuming that all problems can be solved by scientific methods. In the *Limits of Science*, one of his last books, Peter Medawar (Nobel Laureate for establishing the feasibility of transplantation) commented:

> That there is indeed a limit upon science is made very likely by the existence of questions that science cannot answer and that no conceivable advance of science would empower it to answer. These are the questions that children ask – the 'ultimate questions' of Karl Popper. I have in mind such questions as:
>
> How did everything begin?
>
> What are we all here for?
>
> What is the point of living?
>
> Doctrinaire positivism – now something of a period piece – dismissed all such questions as non-questions or pseudoquestions such as only simpletons ask and only charlatans of one kind or another profess to be able to answer. This peremptory dismissal leaves one empty and dissatisfied because the questions make sense to those who ask them, and the answers, to those who try to give them; but whatever else may be in dispute, it would be universally agreed that it is not to science that we should look for answers.[26]

It is ironic but perhaps not unexpected that there has been a tendency among some Christians to argue along parallel lines to the claims of 'restricted scientists', that there is such a thing as a normal Christian life or an ideal path to sanctification for all Christians. We profess there is salvation only in Christ, but then we must go on to recognize our differences within the church:

> We who are united with Christ, though many,
> form one body, and belong to one another as its
> limbs and organs. Let us use the different gifts
> allotted to each of us by God's grace: the gift of
> inspired utterance, for example, let us use in pro-
> portion to our faith; the gift of administration to
> administer; the gift of teaching to teach; the gift of
> counselling to counsel (Rom. 12:5–8, REB).

In introducing a book of essays decrying enforced Christian stereotyping, John Stott wrote:

> We detest totalitarian regimes that permit neither
> dissidents nor deviants. A so-called freedom that
> results in drab uniformity is a contradiction in
> terms. It is also an affront to our human dignity.
> We yearn for freedom because we sense that this is
> what it means to be a human being. We should be
> free. We could be free. Indeed, we *are* free, for we
> are responsible moral agents, capable of making
> our own choices and decisions.[27]

E. J. Calabrese[28] claims that the word 'ecogenetics' was coined by G. J. Brewer in a 1971 editorial in the *American Journal of Human Genetics*. This may be correct, although the unelided term (ecological genetics) was certainly in common use well before 1970. The first edition of E. B. Ford's *Ecological Genetics*[29] was published in 1964, and planned (as Ford described in his preface) in 1928. Perhaps 1971 marks the time when ecological genetics came of age and began to be recognized as significant in medicine. Brewer linked 'the tremendous genetic variability in natural populations such as man' with 'an environmental crisis of such proportions that our very existence is threatened', and suggested 'we may be seeing the first tip of the iceberg of "ecogenetics".'[30] The important point for us as doctors is to recognize that we are the unique product of a unique genome living in a personal environment. No longer is it sufficient to regard our patients as mass-produced humans released from a nine-month assembly line into a common Skinner's box. Aldous Huxley's *Brave New World* still exerts an enormous influence on the subconscious of educated Westerners.

Ecology

The systematic study of variation is ecological (or population) genetics. (Non-inherited variation is not excluded, because inherited factors determine the norms and extent of variation.) It is improper, however, to separate the organisms which vary from the environment (or 'context') in which they dwell.[31] The emerging discipline of population biology recognizes this by combining genetics with ecology.[32] Ecology as a science went through a difficult period in the 1970s and 1980s when it was commonly used as a synonym for environmental activism. Fortunately, the activists now call themselves 'Greens'. In Britain, the Ecology Party (founded in 1973) changed its name in 1985 to the Green Party. Consequently the word 'ecology' has now been largely rehabilitated as a legitimate scientific enterprise.

The term 'ecology' was originally coined by Ernst Haeckel (1834–1919) in 1866 because 'biology' had become so limited as to exclude physiology and embryology. He wanted to rescue 'biology' as a general term. Ecology is literally the science or study of the place or dwelling (*ecos* or *oikos*), while economy is the management or law of the place. Haeckel regarded ecology as a branch of physiology, and this has remained the German (and North American) emphasis. In Britain, ecology (and the British Ecological Society – the oldest ecology society in the world, founded 1913) sprang from a natural history tradition, and has retained a more pragmatic base than in some other countries.

Ecology is a search for pattern, with its basic problem 'Why is what where?' This is such a wide-ranging question that it is not surprising that the subject has been bedevilled by changing fashions and disagreements about whether its development should be driven by models, ecosystem studies, energetics, physiological understanding, or what.[33]

Historically, the cause of pattern was found in mythology or theology, linked to a notion of a 'balance of nature' upheld by some sort of divine providence.[34] This derives from a common medieval belief that nature can be regarded as a super-organism or macrocosm analogous to the microcosm of the individual. The assumption of a natural or ecological balance still persists in popular writings and political rhetoric, although there is no evidence for it, beyond various homeostatic mechanisms which regulate particular interactions (for example, density-dependent limitations on fertility in many species, or buffering of acidity in lakes). J. E. Lovelock's Gaia hypothesis is a good example of a postulated feedback mechanism on a large scale. In itself, it is a legitimate scientific hypothesis, susceptible to test by experiment,[35] but it has been hijacked by non-scientists as a mystical reality with unacceptable implications to many people.

Gaian and similar fantasies have scared many orthodox Christians because of the overt animist and polytheist claims of 'Green religion'. There is (or should be) a clear distinction between the clear teaching of Scripture on stewardship, and earth-centred (or creation-centred) teachings of oneness between earth, life and mankind. The Bible message is that the earth belongs to God by creation, redemption and sustainment (Jb. 38–41; Ps. 24:1, 3; 1 Cor. 10:26; Col. 1:16–20), and we are his stewards (Gn. 1:26, 9:16, 17; Lk. 12:42–48, 19:12–27, 20:9–18).[36] For many Greens, Mother Earth has replaced the Father God.[37] The American Roman Catholic priest Thomas Berry believes 'The ultimate custody of the earth belongs to the earth ... As humans we need to recognize the limitation in our capacity to deal with these comprehensive issues of earth functioning.'[38] Similarly, the Jesuit Sean MacDonagh has written:

> Rather than acting as a parasite, human beings must now assume their proper function as the head and mind of Gaia and thereby optimize the conditions necessary for life on earth. We carry

within ourselves, and every life-form carries within itself, a unique manifestation of the ultimate mystery of life.[39]

The 'new consciousness', the 'Aquarian conspiracy', the New Age, and other syncretistic movements are relevant here for two reasons: the discredit they bring to science in general and ecology in particular; and the link between them and 'holistic health'. A critique of holistic health and the New Age is given by Derek Munday in Chapter 4 of this volume. For the present all we need to do is to emphasize that, while the factors which contribute to health and disease in the orthodox sense are not completely known, there is no proof whatsoever for any of the underlying assumptions of holistic healing.[40] The New Age definition of health as 'a dynamic and harmonious equilibrium of all elements and forces making up and surrounding a human being'[41] is seductive but largely meaningless.

New Age holistic healing is, in part at least, a reaction against the sterility of so-called 'scientific medicine', but both are extremes and ecology in the narrow sense contributes to neither. Notwithstanding, ecology is pertinent in understanding health in the sense of 'strength to be human', and its most relevant concept is that of habitat or niche.[42]

Niche

In formal terms, a niche is a multidimensional utilization distribution, defining a population's use of resources ordered along axes such as prey size or feeding site. Originally the idea of niche was used simply to refer to the place of an organism or population in the community; as the concept has developed, it has come to include a comparison (or quantification) of the number of species in a niche and the stresses acting on them. Unfortunately 'stress' tends to be regarded as an individual response (particularly by mammalian physiologists) rather than the external force or forces which produce the response. R. K. Koehn and B. L. Bayne define ecological stress as 'anything which reduces fitness',[43] and have developed their ideas in terms of a dynamic and integrated response, involving all levels of functional complexity, potentially changing over time and liable to be neutralized by homeostatic physiological compensation. This permits energy gains and losses to be measured and represented in the form of energy equations, and ecological pressures to be expressed in physiological terms.

The significance of stress considered in this way is that it can be used as a frame for what may be called 'natural history observations' (or, translated into medical language, clinical history). T. R. E. Southwood has listed the five main problem areas in the life of an individual (physiological adaptation to inclement physical conditions, defence to avoid death by predation, food harvesting and somatic development, reproductive activities, and escape in time or space) as 'combinations of tactics determined by the potential of the genome ... for which selection can act. Each of these involves a different amount of risk (i.e. a "trade-off") between alternative courses of actions; each of them involves investment in a trait.'[44]

These five situations are all ones where differential fitness may occur. They provide the basis for a model or templet of the environment, where an individual can find a place and reduce the stress on him or herself. These concepts are only just beginning to find a place in biological ecology, and there is no reason why they should not be applied to humans. When the railway from Islington to Camberwell was opened a hundred years ago, Matthew Arnold enquired what was the value of a railway which enabled one to pass 'from a dismal and illiberal life in Islington to a dismal and illiberal life in Camberwell'. He was in fact exploring the question of niche in the same (albeit more tentative) way that ecologists do nowadays. There is almost certainly no such thing as an ideal human environment. As G. Rattray Taylor has expressed it,[45] an assembly line worker in a poet's environment is likely to be as miserable as a poet in an assembly line worker's environment. Health must involve ideally the opportunity for every individual to choose an appropriate niche.

Lebret[46] has distinguished three kinds of human needs:

Subsistence – those things we must have to maintain life: food, clothing, shelter, healthcare, and education.

Comfort and facilities – *e.g.* transport, labour-saving devices *etc.* At times these may be luxuries, but usually they are not.

Transcendence – goods that cannot be measured or priced, but are no less real. They include religion and friendship. Without such goods our lives would be little different from those of non-human animals.

These 'needs' bound the human habitat; within them, we all have to find our own niche. An unfavourable niche leads to stress. Stress is not intrinsically bad, but excessive stress is debilitating and draining. An acceptable amount of stress (which can act, *inter alia*, as a healthy stimulant) is a matter for personal and/or clinical judgment. The correct niche for an individual, however, is not a matter of social or political (or medical) provision; it is a matter of personal choice based on an individual's physical and spiritual interplay with the environment – a question both of calculation and idiosyncrasy.

The role of the doctor in this is as an enabler, alert to markers of disease (now being employed on a much wider scale than their early use as indicators of genetic damage by radiation, which were too rare to be of use for individual cases)[47] and to the possible dangers from apparently correct treatments.[48] It is not yet possible to measure and balance all the relevant factors which affect human health – it may never be possible. The important fact to recognize is that our world is much, much more than 'the backdrop to God's glory'. We are unique interactors with an incredibly complex set of influences. When we put the genetic variety of individual body-souls together with environmental heterogeneity, our responses are personal to ourselves. And our humanness, and therefore our health, is the result of these responses.

Environmental concern: paradise to pollution

So far we have regarded our environment as almost abstract, a complex of hazards and rewards that influences our food, fertility and future. Recent years, however, have seen an unprecedented growth of awareness that increasing numbers of us are dependent on a degrading environment, and that we are – as a species – responsible for this deterioration. In crude terms, we are running out of world.[49] In earlier times the response to environmental problems – whether local agriculture, or climate change – was migration into empty territory. Now, though, most habitable land is occupied; most of us have to cope where we are.

Environmental pressures only really began to become acute in Britain as a consequence of urban growth and industrialization in the nineteenth century. As late as 1790, four in every five people lived in the country; 40 years later, one in every two lived in a town. Any common land near an expanding industrial town offered tempting sites for building. An Act of 1836 provided that lands within a certain distance of London and other large towns should not be inclosed, but the major step had to wait for a century and a Royal Commission on the Distribution of the Industrial Population (1937–40). This led in due course to the current structure of planning laws, and to the establishment of a statutory Countryside Commission and Nature Conservancy.

In 1962, the American Rachel Carson's book *Silent Spring*[50] drew attention to the insidious dangers of persistent pesticides. In 1967, the wreck of the Liberian oil tanker *Torry Canyon* off Land's End alerted the British public to the ever-present risks of oil pollution. In 1970 the British Government set up a Royal Commission on Environmental Pollution, which remains the only standing

Royal Commission on science. It has published influential Reports on (among other topics) Estuarine Pollution (1972), Nuclear Power (1976), Agriculture and Pollution (1979), Lead in the Environment (1983), Managing Waste (1985), and the Release of Genetically Engineered Organisms to the Environment (1989).

In 1972 a computer simulation carried out at Massachusetts Institute of Technology was published under the title *The Limits of Growth*.[51] Its message was that the economic and industrial systems of affluent countries would collapse about the year 2100 unless action was taken to ensure that birth rate does not exceed death rate, and that capital investment equals capital depreciation. If these conditions were met, a 'stabilized world model' would result.

The MIT model was taken as the basis for a 'Blueprint for Survival', issued in the magazine *Ecologist* in 1972, and endorsed by a group of leading ecologists. Its argument was that the non-renewable resources which provided the raw materials for energy generation for much of industry were threatened with drastic depletion within a time-span that ordinarily commands political attention, as a result of exponential increase in consumption and population growth; and the waste which accompanies this exploitation threatens the processes which sustain human life. The authors of the manifesto proposed a radical reordering of priorities, with industrial societies converting themselves into stable societies characterized by minimum disruption of ecological processes, maximum conservation of materials and energy, and static populations. *The Times* reacted with a first leader on 14 January 1972, headed 'the prophets may be right'.

The calculations of the *Limits of Growth* and the 'Blueprint', however, were rendered void within a few years by the Arab–Israeli wars and a massive increase in the price of fossil fuels. Lord Ashby (who had been first chairman of the Royal Commission on Environmental Pollution) took *A Second Look at Doom*, speaking of the ominous instability of man-made ecosystems. He pointed out that

171

> if we experience a shift in the balance of economic
> power between nations which own resources and
> nations which need those resources to keep their
> economies going, one sure consequence would be
> an increase in tension in the social systems on both
> sides ... The tempting way to resolve these ten-
> sions is by autocracy and force.[52]

In other words, the period of good-mannered agreement over the use of resources probably would not hold.
Conservation was on the international agenda, but it
required a change of attitudes as well as an intellectual
assent to impending problems.

The next major event was the issuing of a *World Conservation Strategy* in 1980 by the International Union for the
Conservation for Nature (IUCN), the World Wildlife Fund
(now the World Wildlife Fund for Nature) and the United
Nations Environmental Programme.[53] It was an unequivocally utilitarian document, stressing that every aspect of
human activity benefits from conservation (and conversely,
was likely to be hindered by environmental mismanage-
ment), and therefore that we have responsibility to contribute positively to our environment. The World
Conservation Strategy required national responses. The
United Kingdom response was published in 1984 under
the title *The Conservation and Development Programme for the
UK* and analysed the situation and required actions under
seven headings: industry, urban, rural, marine and coastal,
international, education, and ethics.

Environmental ethics

Ethical issues have come increasingly to the fore in the past
decade. A successor to the World Conservation Strategy was
published in 1991 under the title *Caring for the Earth*,
emphasizing the absolute need for sustainable development
(a theme spelt out by the World Commission on Environment and Development in the Brundtland Report), and the

moral as well as the economic and political challenges involved in achieving this. In the Declaration of Fontaine-bleau issued to mark its 40th anniversary, IUCN pro-claimed, 'If humanity is to find the right way forward, it must base its advance on a code of values that is less aggressive and more caring for the earth.'

Meanwhile a Conference of the Economic Summit Nations in 1989[54] called for a 'Code of Environmental Practice', and this was issued in 1990. The Code recognized that

> we are dependent upon our environment, yet capable of manipulating and managing it to a variable extent; we are simultaneously apart from, yet part of our physical, anthropogenic and social environment, which may stimulate or adversely stress us. A high quality of life is a legitimate aspiration for all, but we must distinguish quality of life from standard of living. Health is best defined positively as wholeness of all aspects of life, not negatively as an absence of disease; health is the strength to be human, with an environment to rejoice in and respond to rather than avoid. The minimum requirement for health is the satisfaction of basic biological and social needs, but a good quality involves also the ability to accept and adjust to change.
>
> Individuals have different priorities, desires and perceived wants, which are determined by social pressures, culture and religion. It is not possible to define more than the basic minimum of health from the environment point of view; it is not dependent upon any specific environmental input, nor defined by a general lack of stress.[55]

The Code starts from the argument that *a.* we depend on the natural world for food, fuel, space and stimulation; the quality of life for people today and for our children tomorrow depends on how successful we are in cherishing that resource; and that *b*. the diversity and beauty of our natural environment are immense gifts with inspirational qualities, and their degradation affects us both materially and spiritually. The Code then sets out an environmental ethic of *stewardship of the living and non-living systems of the earth in order to maintain their sustainability for present and future, allowing development with equity*. It asserts that health and quality of life for humankind are ultimately dependent on this.

Acceptance of such an ethic entails characteristics common to good citizens, states and corporations everywhere (responsibility in strengthening good management and restraining present actions; freedom for both society and future generations to have no limits on their environmental decisions; justice, for individuals of all nations, recognizing that some carry environmental burdens which may require help from the more privileged; sensitivity; awareness; acceptance; truthfulness). Acceptance also involves the recognition of obligations, which mean discipline and self-restraint.

This is not the place to expound or justify this ethic in detail. Clearly it is compatible with the Christian doctrine of environmental stewardship, and meshes intimately with the concept of health espoused by the European Charter and explained in previous sections of this chapter. In opening a series of meetings at Windsor on 'the Christian Attitude to Nature',[56] the Duke of Edinburgh asked 'There must be a moral as well as a practical argument for environmental conservation: what is it?' The answer is responsible stewardship; the world is made and redeemed by God and entrusted to us, we are accountable to him. So once more we come to a holism which is based on God's creation and authority, and not at all on the blurring of boundaries desired by New Age adherents. Health is being in God's place at God's time, not merely having the luck or making the effort to avoid disease.

Evolution

On a number of occasions in this essay I have referred to humankind as a special creation in God's image, but also as a physically evolved creature genetically kin to the great apes. The idea of evolution remains anathema to some Christians. From the point of view of a proper understanding of health, does it matter whether physically we have evolved or not?

The easy answer is that health is an individual matter, and species history is irrelevant. There are two reasons, however, for this being too glib an answer.

Firstly, if we are assumed to be a special creation in body, mind and spirit, we can believe in a God remote (and by implication even ineffectual) in this world. The divine watchmaker of Archdeacon Paley retired from his creation to oversee it from his heavenly eyrie, perhaps occasionally adjusting the works but essentially a separated and distant watchmaker. The concept presented in this essay is a world indwelt, maintained and sustained by God's power; this is very different. The Bible presents God as an immanent power, overruling and controlling natural forces. If he really is in charge of everyday occurrences (as we accept when we pray), there is no reason why he could not have worked through the evolutionary processes of selection, mutation, differentiation and so on. The writer to the Hebrews tells us that it is '*by faith* we understand that the universe was formed at God's command' (Heb. 11:3), not by processes we can discover by study. There is no way that we can prove that God is (or has been) at work in creation. God is a God, however, who reveals himself by works of nature and of grace. If we believe this and believe that he is at work in our daily lives, the weight of evidence is that God is at work through evolution rather than being merely a 'non-resident landowner'.

At root, the disagreement between Christians who are evolutionists and those who deny evolution is a matter of the mechanism of God's working: either God worked through natural processes or he did not.[57] This is in theory (but not in practice) a fairly trivial argument because, as Job discovered after extensive enquiry, it is never possible to *prove* that any action is God's. The essential doctrine is that God is sovereign in this world, and therefore can use whatever methods he chooses.

There is a second consequence, however, of rejecting evolution, and that is that Christians have never taken the doctrine of creation as seriously as they should have done. Consequently we have tended to lose the fear and awe of the Lord, which is the beginning of wisdom. This is much more serious.

Health and holiness

The Bible links obedience to God with material prosperity and good health (*e.g.* Lv. 26:3ff.; Dt. 28:1ff.). Such teaching appears naive to most of us (who have no reason to doubt that, for example, plentiful harvests depend more on soil, seed and weather than the holiness of the farmer). It is reminiscent of prosperity theology, now unfashionable following scandals involving some of its more prominent practitioners in the USA. We should, however, beware of ignoring this Scriptural teaching. Herein lies one of the elements of health and wholeness. If we are to have the strength to be human, we must be in God's place and on his way. The answer to our environmental problems is not in the first place lifestyle, nor is it primarily environmental activism, but rather the answer is a recognition and acknowledgment of God as Lord over the whole of his world. As we accept this saving power in our lives, we need also to recognize that *all things* hold together in Christ (Col. 1:17) – our ecological niche as well as our body, our social relationships as well as our biochemical mechanisms. God has become too small for many people; he has been squeezed into the ever decreasing gaps of knowledge. That is the trouble with much 'scientific medicine' nowadays, even when practised by Christians. We can treat disease with scant regard for its context. We may even achieve good results and acceptance as a clever doctor. But good health – and surely good medicine should be directed to good health – 'requires a clean and harmonious environment in which physical, psychological, social and aesthetic factors are all given their due importance'. So states the European Charter on Environment and Health. We have come full circle.

Notes and references

1 The full text of the Charter is printed as an Appendix to this chapter.
2 World Commission on Environment and Development, *Our Common Future* (Oxford University Press, 1987), p. xi.
3 D. MacKay, *Brains, Machines and Persons* (Collins, 1980).
4 S. A. Barnett, *Biology and Freedom* (Cambridge, 1988).
5 K. Barth, *Church Dogmatics* (T. & T. Clark, 1961), III/4, p. 189.
6 E. Brunner, *Man in Revolt* (Lutterworth, 1939), pp. 96–97.
7 C. F. D. Moule, *Man and Nature in the New Testament* (Athlone Press, 1964), p. 5.
8 R. J. Berry, 'What to believe about miracles', *Nature* 322 (1986), pp. 321–322.
9 See S. J. Gould, *The Mismeasure of Man* (Norton, 1981).
10 J. B. S. Haldane, *Heredity and Politics* (Allen & Unwin, 1938), pp. 179–180.
11 G. Dean, *The Porphyrias* (Pitman Medical, 1963).
12 See, *e.g.*, C. R. Scriver, W. S. Sly, A. L. Beaudet, and D. Valle (eds.), *Metabolic Basis of Inherited Disease* (McGraw-Hill, [6]1989).
13 See C. A. Clarke, *Genetics for the Clinician* (Blackwell, [2]1964); R. J. Berry, *Inheritance and Natural History* (Collins, 1977).
14 R. A. Fisher, *Genetical Theory of Natural Selection* (Clarendon Press, 1930).
15 J. B. S. Haldane, 'Disease and evolution', *La Ricerca Scientifica, Supplement* 19 (1949), pp. 68–76; see also W. C. Boyd, *Genetics and the Races of Man* (Blackwell, 1950).
16 See, *e.g.*, G. M. Howe, *Man, Environment and Disease in Britain* (David & Charles, 1972).
17 See B. Kellock, *The Fibre Man* (Lion, 1985), pp. 134–164.
18 A. C. Allison, 'Protection afforded by the sickle-cell trait against subtertian malarial infection', *British Medical Journal* i (1954), pp. 290–294.

19 See, *e.g.*, R. J. Berry, 'Genetical factors in the aetiology of multiple sclerosis', *Acta Neurologica Scandinavica* 45 (1969), pp. 459–483.

20 H. Harris, 'Enzyme polymorphisms in man', *Proceedings of the Royal Society of London*, series B, 164 (1966), pp. 298–310.

21 R. C. Lewontin and J. L. Hubby, 'A molecular approach to the study of genetic heterozygosity in natural populations. II. Amount of variation and degree of heterozygosity in natural populations of *Drosophila pseudoobscura*', *Genetics* 54 (1966), pp. 595–609.

22 I am aware that affirmation of evolution is still regarded by some Christians as a sign of heresy. It should be clear from the discussion about God's image in us on pp. 157–158 that the *essential human* part of mankind is not genetic but divine, and there should be no problems for Christians to accept that we *physically* share a common ancestor with the apes (see R. J. Berry, 'The Theology of DNA, *Anvil* 4 (1987), pp. 39–49; and *God and Evolution*, Hodder & Stoughton, 1988). A further digression on the relation between evolution and God's creation occurs below (pp. 175–176).

23 R. J. Berry, 'Where biology meets; or how science advances', *Biological Journal of the Linnean Society* 32 (1987), pp. 257–274.

24 C. F. A. Pantin, *Relations between the Sciences* (Cambridge University Press, 1968), p. 18.

25 F. J. Ayala, Introduction, in F. J. Ayala and T. Dobzhansky (eds.), *Studies in the Philosophy of Biology* (Macmillian, 1974), pp. vii-xvi; A. R. Peacocke, *God and the New Biology* (Dent, 1986), pp. 5–20.

26 P. Medawar, *The Limits of Science* (Harper & Row, 1984), p. 66. In her autobiography, Medawar's widow describes the theme of this book as stressing 'science should not be expected to provide solutions to problems such as the purpose of life or the existence of God, for which it was unfitted' (J. Medawar, *A Very Decided Preference*, Oxford University Press, 1990, p. 220).

27 J. R. W. Stott (ed.), *Free to be Different* (Marshalls, 1984).

28 E. J. Calabrese, *Ecogenetics* (Wiley, 1984).

29 E. B. Ford, *Ecological Genetics* (Methuen, 1964).

30 G. J. Brewer, 'Human ecology, an expanding role for the human geneticist', *American Journal of Human Genetics* 23 (1971), pp. 92–94.

31 R. J. Berry, 'Scientific natural history: a key base to ecology', *Biological Journal of the Linnean Society* 32 (1987), pp. 17–29;

idem, 'Conservation genetics: ecological and genetical interactions', in O. T. Sandlund, K. Hindar and A. H. D. Brown (eds.), *Conservation of Biodiversity for Sustainable Development* (Scandinavian University Press, 1992), pp. 107–123.

32 See, *e.g.*, E. O. Wilson and W. H. Bossert, *Primer of Population Biology* (Sinauer, 1971).

33 R. J. Berry, 'Ecology: where genes and geography meet', *Journal of Animal Ecology* 58 (1989), pp. 733–759.

34 F. N. Egerton, 'Changing concepts in the balance of nature', *Quarterly Review of Biology* 48 (1973), pp. 322–350.

35 L. Margulis and J. E. Lovelock, 'Gaia and geognosy', pp. 1–30 in M. B. Rambler, L. Margulis and R. Fester, *Global Ecology* (Academic Press, 1989); J. E. Lovelock, 'Gaia', *Journal of the Marine Biology Association* 69 (1989), pp. 746–758; J. C. A. Craik, 'The Gaia hypothesis – fact or fancy?', *Journal of the Marine Biology Association* 69 (1989), pp. 759–768.

36 See R. J. Berry, *Ecology and Ethics* (Inter-Varsity Press, 1972); R. Moss, *The Earth in Our Hands* (Inter-Varsity Press, 1982); R. Attfield, *The Ethics of Environmental Concern* (Blackwell, 1983).

37 D. R. Groothius, *Unmasking the New Age* (Inter-Varsity Press, 1986), p. 48.

38 T. Berry in *Cross Currents* 37 (1987), pp. 178–224, *q.v.* p. 186.

39 S. McDonagh, *To Care for the Earth* (Geoffrey Chapman, 1986), p. 88.

40 This is not to pass any judgment on whether or not 'miraculous healing' ever occurs. My concern is the theoretical basis claimed for some beliefs.

41 A. Weil, *Health and Healing* (Houghton Mifflin, 1983), p. 51.

42 T. W. Schoener, 'The ecological niche', in J. M. Cherrett (ed.), *Ecological Concepts* (Blackwell, 1989), pp. 79–113.

43 R. K. Koehn and B. L. Bayne, 'Towards a physiological and genetical understanding of the energetics of the stress response', *Biological Journal of the Linnean Society* 37 (1989), pp. 157–171.

44 T. R. E. Southwood, 'Tactics, strategies and templets', *Oikos* 52 (1988), pp. 3–18.

45 G. Rattray Taylor, *Rethink: a paraprimitive solution* (Secker & Warburg, 1972).

46 See D. Goulet, *The Cruel Choice: a new concept in the theory of development* (University Press of America, 1985), pp. 215–235.

47 P. A. Schulte, 'A conceptual framework for the validation and use of biological markers', *Environmental Research* 48 (1989), pp. 129–144.

48 An excellent example of this is the treatment of childhood leukaemia by 6-mercaptopurine (L. Lennard, J. S. Lilleyman, J. Van Loon and R. M. Weinshilboum, 'Genetic variation in response to 6-mercaptopurine for childhood acute lympho-blastic leukaemia, *Lancet* 336, 1990, pp. 225–229). There is considerable inherited variation in enzymatic transformation of this drug to its active form, and it is not sufficient merely to prescribe a 'normal dose'. Conversely, the drug is much more effective than an assessment in a random trial would indicate, since a random group of patients will contain those who will respond to treatment and those who still suffer toxic side-effects.

49 J. A. McNeely, K. R. Miller, W. V. Reid, R. A. Mittermeier and T. B. Werner, *Conserving the World's Biological Diversity* (International Union for the Conservation of Nature and Natural Resources, World Resources Institute, Conservation International, World Wildlife Fund – US and World Bank, 1990).

50 R. Carson, *Silent Spring* (Houghton Mifflin, 1962; Hamish Hamilton, 1963).

51 D. H. Meadows, D. L. Meadows, J. Randers and W. W. Behrens, *The Limits to Growth* (Earth Island, 1972).

52 E. Ashby, *A Second Look at Doom*, Twenty-first Fawley Foundation Lecture (University of Southampton, 1975), p. 16.

53 World Conservation Strategy (International Union for the Conservation of Nature, 1980).

54 P. Bordeau, P. M. Fassella, and A. Teller (eds.), *Environmental Ethics. Man's Relationship with Nature. Interactions with Science* (Commission of European Communities, 1990).

55 The Code is reproduced in R. J. Berry (ed.), *Environmental Dilemmas: Ethics and Decisions* (Chapman & Hall, 1993), pp. 253–264, *q.v.* p. 255; for its background, see R. J. Berry, 'Environmental knowledge, attitudes and action: a code of practice', *Science and Public Affairs* 5 (1990), pp. 13–23.

56 Duke of Edinburgh and M. Mann, *Survival or Extinction: A Christian Attitude to the Environment* (Michael Russell, 1989).

57 R. J. Berry, *God and Evolution* (Hodder & Stoughton, 1988).

Appendix to Chapter Seven

European Charter on Environment and Health

First European Conference on Environment and Health,
Frankfurt, 7–8 December 1989

Preamble

In the light of WHO's strategy for health for all in Europe, the
report of the World Commission on Environment and Development and the related Environmental Perspective to the Year 2000
and Beyond (resolutions 42/187 and 42/186 of the United
Nations General Assembly) and World Health Assembly resolu-
tion WHA42.26,

■ *Recognizing* the dependence of human health on a wide range
of crucial environmental factors;

■ *Stressing* the vital importance of preventing health hazards by
protecting the environment;

■ *Acknowledging* the benefits to health and wellbeing that accrue
from a clean and harmonious environment;

■ *Encouraged* by the many examples of positive achievement in
the abatement of pollution and the restoration of a healthy
environment;

■ *Mindful* that the maintenance and improvement of health and
wellbeing require a sustainable system of development;

■ *Concerned* at the ill-considered use of natural resources and
man-made products in ways liable to damage the environment
and endanger health;

■ *Considering* the international character of many environmental
and health issues and the interdependence of nations and
individuals in these matters;

■ *Conscious* of the fact that since developing countries are faced with major environmental problems, there is a need for global cooperation;

■ *Responding* to the specific characteristics of the European Region, and notably its large population, intensive industrialization and dense traffic;

■ *Taking into account* existing international instruments (such as agreements on protection of the ozone layer) and other initiatives relating to the environment and health,

the Ministers of the Environment and of Health of the Member States of the European Region of WHO, meeting together for the first time at Frankfurt-am-Main on 7 and 8 December 1989, have adopted the attached European Charter on Environment and Health and have accordingly agreed upon the principles and strategies laid down therein as a firm commitment to action. In view of its environmental mandate, the Commission of the European Communities was specially invited to participate and acting on behalf of the Community also adopted the Charter as a guideline for future action by the Community in areas which lie within Community competence.

Entitlements and Responsibilities

1. *Every individual* is entitled to:

   • an environment conducive to the highest attainable level of health and wellbeing;

   • information and consultation on the state of the environment, and on plans, decisions and activities likely to affect both the environment and health;

   • participation in the decision-making process.

2. *Every individual* has a responsibility to contribute to the protection of the environment, in the interests of his or her own health and the health of others.

3. *All sections* of society are responsible for protecting the environment and health as an intersectoral matter involving many disciplines; their respective duties should be clarified.

4. *Every public authority* and agency at different levels, in its daily work, should cooperate with other sectors in order to resolve problems of the environment and health.

5. *Every government and public authority* has the responsibility to protect the environment and to promote human health within the area under its jurisdiction, and to ensure that activities under its jurisdiction or control do not cause damage to

human health in other states. Furthermore, each shares the common responsibility for safeguarding the global environment.

6. *Every public and private body* should assess its activities and carry them out in such a way as to protect peoples' health from harmful effects related to the physical, chemical, biological, microbiological and social environments. Each of these bodies should be accountable for its actions.

7. *The media* play a key role in promoting awareness and a positive attitude towards protection of health and the environment. They are entitled to adequate and accurate information and should be encouraged to communicate this information effectively to the public.

8. *Nongovernmental organizations* also play an important role in disseminating information to the public and promoting public awareness and response.

Principles for Public Policy

1. Good health and wellbeing require a clean and harmonious environment in which physical, psychological, social and aesthetic factors are all given their due importance. The environment should be regarded as a resource for improving living conditions and increasing wellbeing.

2. The preferred approach should be to promote the principle of 'prevention is better than cure'.

3. The health of every individual, especially those in vulnerable and high-risk groups, must be protected. Special attention should be paid to disadvantaged groups.

4. Action on problems of the environment and health should be based on the best available scientific information.

5. New policies, technologies and developments should be introduced with prudence and not before appropriate prior assessment of the potential environmental and health impact. There should be a responsibility to show that they are not harmful to health or the environment.

6. The health of individuals and communities should take clear precedence over considerations of economy and trade.

7. All aspects of socioeconomic development that relate to the impact of the environment on health and wellbeing must be considered.

8. The entire flow of chemicals, materials, products and waste should be managed in such a way as to achieve optimal use of

natural resources and to cause minimal contamination.

9. Governments, public authorities and private bodies should aim at both preventing and reducing adverse effects caused by potentially hazardous agents and degraded urban and rural environments.

10. Environmental standards need to be continually reviewed to take account of new knowledge about the environment and health and of the effects of future economic development. Where applicable such standards should be harmonized.

11. The principle should be applied whereby every public and private body that causes or may cause damage to the environment is made financially responsible ('the polluter pays' principle).

12. Criteria and procedures to quantify, monitor and evaluate environmental and health damage should be further developed and implemented.

13. Trade and economic policies and development assistance programmes affecting the environment and health in foreign countries should comply with all the above principles. Export of environmental and health hazards should be avoided.

14. Development assistance should promote sustainable development and the safeguarding and improvement of human health as one of its integral components.

Strategic Elements

1. The environment should be managed as a positive resource for human health and wellbeing.

2. In order to protect health, comprehensive strategies are required, including, *inter alia*, the following elements:

   (a) The responsibilities of public and private bodies for implementing appropriate measures should be clearly defined at all levels.

   (b) Control measures and other tools should be applied, as appropriate, to reduce risks to health and wellbeing from environmental factors. Fiscal, administrative and economic instruments and land-use planning have a vital role to play in promoting environmental conditions conducive to health and wellbeing and should be used for that purpose.

   (c) Better methods of prevention should be introduced as knowledge expands, including the use of the most appropriate and cost-effective technologies and, if necessary, the imposition of bans.

(d) Low-impact technology and products and the recycling and reuse of wastes should be encouraged. Changes should be made, as necessary, in raw materials, production processes and waste management techniques.

(e) High standards in management and operations should be followed to ensure that appropriate technologies and best practices are applied, that regulations and guidance are adhered to, and that accidents and human failures are avoided.

(f) Appropriate regulations should be promulgated; they should be both enforceable and enforced.

(g) Standards should be set on the basis of the best available scientific information. The cost and benefit of action or lack of action and feasibility may also have to be assessed but in all cases risks should be minimized.

(h) Comprehensive strategies should be developed that take account of the risks to human health and the environment arising from chemicals. These strategies should include, *inter alia*, registration procedures for new chemicals and systematic examination of existing chemicals.

(i) Contingency planning should be undertaken to deal with all types of serious accident, including those with transfrontier consequences.

(j) Information systems should be strengthened to support monitoring of the effectiveness of measures taken, trend analysis, priority-setting and decision-making.

(k) Environmental impact assessment should give greater emphasis to health aspects. Individuals and communities directly affected by the quality of a specific environment should be consulted and involved in managing that environment.

3. Medical and other relevant disciplines should be encouraged to pay greater attention to all aspects of environmental health. Environmental toxicology and environmental epidemiology are key tools of environmental health research and should be strengthened and further developed as special disciplines within the Region.

4. Interdisciplinary research programmes in environmental epidemiology with the aim of clarifying links between the environment and health should be encouraged and strength-

ened at regional, national and international levels.

5. The health sector should have responsibility for epidemiological surveillance through data collection, compilation, analysis and risk assessment of the health impact of environmental factors and for informing other sectors of society and the general public of trends and priorities.

6. National and international programmes of multidisciplinary training as well as the provision of health education and information for public and private bodies should be encouraged and strengthened.

Priorities

1. Governments and other public authorities, without prejudice to the importance of problem areas specific to their respective countries, the European Community and other intergovernmental organizations, as appropriate, should pay particular attention to the following urgent issues of the environment and health at local, regional, national and international levels and will endeavour to take action on them:

   global disturbances to the environment, such as the destruction of the ozone layer and climatic change;

   urban development, planning and renewal to protect health and promote wellbeing;

   safe and adequate drinking-water supplies on the basis of the WHO *Guidelines for drinking-water quality* together with **hygienic waste disposal** for all urban and rural communities;

   water quality, in relation to surface, ground, coastal and recreational waters;

   microbiological and chemical safety of food;

   environment and health impact of

   ● **various energy options**

   ● **transport,** especially road transport

   ● **agricultural practices,** including the use of fertilizers and pesticides, and waste disposal;

   air quality, on the basis of the WHO *Air quality guidelines for Europe*, especially in relation to oxides of sulfur and nitrogen, the photochemical oxidants ('summer smog') and volatile organic compounds;

indoor air quality (residential, recreational and occupational), including the effects of radon, passive smoking and chemicals;

persistent chemicals and those causing chronic effects;

hazardous wastes, including management, transport and disposal;

biotechnology, in particular genetically modified organisms;

contingency planning for and in response to accidents and disasters;

cleaner technologies as preventive measures.

2. In addressing all of these priorities, the importance of **intersectoral environmental planning and community management** to generate optimal health and wellbeing should be borne in mind.

3. **Health promotion** should be added to health protection so as to induce the adoption of healthy lifestyles in a clean and harmonious environment.

4. It should be recognized that some urgent problems require direct and immediate **international cooperation and joint efforts.**

The Way Forward

1. **Member States of the European Region should:**

   (a) take all necessary steps to reverse negative trends as soon as possible and to maintain and increase the health-related improvements already taking place. In particular, they should make every effort to implement WHO's regional strategy for health for all as it concerns the environment and health;

   (b) strengthen collaboration among themselves and, where appropriate, with the European Community and with other inter-governmental bodies, on mutual and transfrontier environmental problems that pose a threat to health;

   (c) ensure that the Charter adopted at this meeting is made widely available in the languages of the European Region.

2. **The WHO Regional Office for Europe is invited to:**

   (a) explore ways of strengthening international mechanisms for assessing potential hazards to health associated with the environment and for developing guidance on their control;

   (b) make a critical study of existing indicators of the effects of the environment on health and, where necessary, develop others that are both specific and effective;

(c) establish a European Advisory Committee on the Environment and Health in consultation with the governments of the countries of the Region;

(d) in collaboration with the governments of the European countries, examine the desirability and feasibility of establishing a European Centre for the Environment and Health or other suitable institutional arrangements, with a view to strengthening collaboration on the health aspects of environmental protection with special emphasis on information systems, mechanisms for exchanging experience and coordinated studies. In such arrangements, cooperation with the United Nations Environment Programme, the United Nations Economic Commission for Europe and other organizations is desirable. Account should be taken of the environmental agency to be established within the European Community.

3. **Member States of the European Region and WHO should:**
   promote the widest possible endorsement of the principles and attainment of the objectives of the Charter.

4. **European Ministers of the Environment and of Health should:**
   meet again within five years to evaluate national and international progress and to endorse specific action plans drawn up by WHO and other international organizations for eliminating the most significant environmental threats to health as rapidly as possible.

Chapter Eight

HEALTH FOR ALL – A WORLDWIDE PERSPECTIVE

Peter Pattisson

General Practitioner, Pembury, Kent
Formerly in the Far East

It is universal human experience that local and personal issues are best understood in the context of wider knowledge and experience. The detail of a fine work of art is seen to best advantage in place in the whole canvas. Individual problems are helped in the family, families in turmoil are strengthened in the community, and nations in crisis are helped by the way in which neighbouring nations have handled similar crises. If this is true in geographical circles it is equally true in historical ones and contemporary problems are frequently resolved in the light of the experience of past generations.

The debates of the previous chapters have necessarily been centred in British and Western experience. The aim of this chapter is to attempt to set these debates and this experience in the wider context of the worldwide contemporary quest for health.

There is no better place to start than with the Alma-Ata Declaration of September 1978. Representatives of 134 nations met under the auspices of WHO and UNICEF at Alma-Ata in South Eastern Soviet Union, close to the Chinese border and drafted a document which has become known as the Alma-Ata Declaration, the slogan of which was 'Health for all by the year 2000'. Now, more than halfway towards the year 2000, the goal still seems a long way from realization. The intention, however, remains and a great deal of international energy is still directed towards the same. In the context of this global intention, the needs of health services in Britain and Western Europe take on a much smaller, and probably more appropriate, perspective. The West argues fiercely over the equitable distribution of resources domestically, but pays scant attention to the yawning chasm between its overall resources and those of many other less advantaged nations.

Western planners debate whether private medical care has an appropriate place in the overall provision, forgetting that in many parts of the world payment for service is the only means of obtaining even the most basic medical service. The global village brings multiple scenes from around the world to Western television screens, but does the manifest gulf between urban and rural provision in so many countries stir more than a passing interest in the minds of Western debaters as they turn once again to endless haggling over domestic issues? The indictment of the Western Church by Amy Carmichael, missionary to Southern India in the earlier years of this century remains, well expressed in her piece, 'The Cry of the Blood'. In it she speaks of Western Christians bitterly engaged in making daisy chains on the edge of a ravine as multitudes rush past them and plunge to oblivion. Fresh excuses are made but little has changed in terms of preoccupation with marginal local issues and culpable neglect of crying worldwide need.

Health for all requires of course a definition of what is

health, and WHO definitions have contained words such as 'health is a state of physical, mental, emotional and spiritual soundness, it is not merely the absence of disease or infirmity, neither is it dependent upon the absence of disability'. A definition such as the above is closely in line with the statement of this book, 'Health: the strength to be human'. It is the inner resource to make appropriate human responses to the physical, mental, emotional and spiritual onslaughts that come upon us from the world around and are an inescapable part of the human condition in the world as it is. This is instinctively and very well understood in most cultures that lack the economic resources and artificial cocoons of Western living.

Contemporary Western concepts of health, understood in the broad definition given at the outset of this book, have tended to want to eliminate all these onslaughts from outside as a necessary precursor to health, and to infect the rest of the world with the illusion that this can be attained. In fact we well know that this is unattainable and probably undesirable for true human vitality. To set this up as the expectation for life is to breed only frustration and disappointment, forces that lead all too often to disruption of harmony and disintegration of true health.

The definition of health at the outset of this book is a very broad one. In the context of worldwide need the present writer would prefer a somewhat narrower one, as more manageable, more realistic and more in line with contemporary usage of the word. Perhaps 'human welfare' is a phrase closer to the sense of this broader definition, though that too carries varying political connotations in different English-speaking cultures. Be that as it may, the majority of the world, when it speaks of health, in its own languages, speaks principally of physical health and, to a lesser extent, mental health. For sure it understands better than most Westerners the need for harmony in relationships with God, with self, with others and with the environment. However, it sees that these relationships will impinge on health for good or ill rather than in themselves constitute health. Almost all world cultures would agree

191

that these relationships make up the essence of humanness, but would see health more in the field of the adequate functioning of physical and mental faculties in order to make appropriate human responses in these areas of relationship.

In looking at some of the issues arising in a worldwide context, this chapter will take the subject matter of each of the preceding chapter headings and focus particularly on the physical and mental (and to a lesser extent, emotional and spiritual), resources necessary to express humanness in the world as it is.

Theology

Modern medical services are the child of *Christian* parents and *Christian* views of life and of what is human. In particular, Christian understandings of the nature of truth and the nature of love have shaped the development of modern Western medicine from its earliest days. Many of the pioneers have been Christians. Whether or not the people involved have been active and personal Christians, however, their thought patterns and approach to life have been shaped by the Christian culture in which they have learned and lived. Thus it is the rigorous application of principles of objective truth, and integrity in applying them, that have lain at the foundation of the development of the modern scientific method and its application in the medical field. At the same time it has been the Christian understanding of love, as exemplified in the parable of the Good Samaritan, that has been the principal stimulus behind all that is best in the development of modern Western medicine.

Where Christians have taken Western medicine overseas to other cultures shaped by other faiths and philosophies, it is these qualities of truth and love that have marked them out. Lord Porritt, writing the foreword to *Heralds of Health*, says of those who went overseas in medical missionary service:

They believed that a patient was an individual and if that individual needed care it involved not only his physical wellbeing but also his mental and spiritual health as well – irrespective of cult, creed or colour. For them there was more to medicine than surgical technology and chemical pharmacology – important as these were, especially in establishing their initial credibility . . . it has taken a century and a half of difficult, dangerous and devoted work, but the responsibilities so bravely shouldered by the early medical missionaries – particularly in China, the Indian subcontinent and Africa – are more and more being accepted by national governments and international organisations.[1]

Elsewhere it has been said 'whether it was leprosaria in India, bush hospitals in Africa, opium refugees in China or medical missions in areas of London, in far-flung corners of the world on every continent it was known for 150 years that if you were poor and sick you went to the Christians because they cared for you'.[2] This was Christian theology worked out at the point of a scalpel.

Such an approach came into conflict with three major strands of thought woven together in different proportions, and producing different patterns, in most of the major faiths and philosophies of the world. The first of these strands is *fatalism*. Illness is part of the divine will and there is nothing we can do except submit. Indeed, to attempt to interfere in the process could be to incur divine wrath. The second of these is *animism*, which sees the origins of ill health in spiritual forces, and the path of restoration to be through appeasement or negation of these forces, often through animal sacrifice. The third strand is that of *relationships*, often seen most strongly in oriental philosophies. Sickness is due to an imbalance of forces disturbing harmonious relationships. Herbal remedies and other medicinal means are methods of restoring this balance and harmony and thus of regaining health.

Christian medical missions found themselves in conflict with these traditional strands of thought. Yet each of them today has a corrective element for contemporary Christian thinking warped by modern Western materialistic humanism.

The *fatalistic* strand reminds us that we cannot control all. We will never produce utopia on earth, and there remains mystery in life. We cannot understand everything in this life. There is much that has to be accepted in the light of divine wisdom.

The *animistic* strand reminds us that there are spiritual causes to much ill health; that sin brings grim rewards, and indeed can open the door to active occult forces.

The emphasis on relationship and harmony that merges closely into the Judaistic concept of shalom reminds us that *relationships* marred by sin can precipitate ill health just as serious ill health can destroy meaningful relationships. The richness, balance and truth of Christian theology is best seen in the context of comparative religion, and nowhere is this more true than in its application to health and medical matters.

Economics

The opening statement of this book declares 'to judge efficiency by financial measures alone is inappropriate, inadequate and immoral'. This may be ethically correct, but like it or not, in most of the world the dominant and overriding factor in decisions relating to health is economic. This is not helped by the North/South divide and the forced export from the 'Christian' West of inappropriate drugs, baby milk, cigarettes and alcoholic products. It is a challenge to Christians in the West to correct some of these injustices, and to Christians serving in many other parts of the world to demonstrate that love can conquer even apparently insurmountable economic barriers. The following incident could have come from one of a hundred different countries, and illustrates the enormity of the economic and moral problems involved:

One sunny Tuesday morning in June among the throng of newcomers to the outpatient clinic was a 16 year old lad from the other side of town. 'I think you'd better come and see him outside,' said the medical assistant. There at the side door of the hospital was a common pushcart with planks laid across it and on top of them a pile of covers from amongst which appeared a sallow face with sunken, frightened eyes. Even before we lifted the covers the smell was repulsive. Removal of the covers revealed an emaciated body with dark, discoloured skin ingrained with dirt. His right thigh was grossly swollen and pouring pus. The slightest movement caused him to cry out with pain, but it was soon clear too that an area about the size of two hands on the back where he was lying was completely ulcerated as a large bed sore. Was it cancer that had ulcerated and become infected? Was it grossly infected osteomyelitis that was the root cause? If it was the former the kindest thing was to allow him to go home to die. If the latter, perhaps we could do something to help. X-ray was blurred and inconclusive. Again we questioned his frightened parents about the story.

Early in March he had developed pain and swelling in his right thigh. He had been admitted to a small 'Christian' hospital in town for 10 days. The family had sold their 2 roomed accommodation to pay the £400 that this had cost, but then the doctor had told them that it was a septic infection of the bone and that an operation would be needed. Money had run out so they took him home. Nearly 3 months mouldering in the back room of the little noodle shop that his parents had managed to acquire had led to the condition in which we found him. His parents had only heard of us the previous day.

We hesitated; could we really help him? Would it be kinder to him to return and die at home?

Faced with the preceding history we felt we couldn't turn him away. We had to put him in a room by himself because of the smell. Turned and dressed twice daily we nursed him mostly naked with a mosquito net to keep the flies off. Although he cried pitiably every time we dressed his wounds, the young man showed great courage and by the grace of God the organisms that were invading him were sensitive to the antibiotics we had. Our medical assistant spent hours working on his hips and knees to regain the movement of then and little by little he regained strength. It was a joyful moment when at last he returned home on crutches.

Christian medicine is more than setting up an institution with a Christian name to it. It requires repeated heartbreaking decisions, heartbreaking because each fresh decision to attempt to rescue one of the crowd of 'harassed and helpless' requires fresh willingness on the part of all the staff to go the second mile. Heartbreaking yes, but heartwarming too as one sees a team of young learners in the school of Discipleship stepping out into the footsteps of the Master.[3]

In the West, we debate resource allocation and have the luxury to sit back and discuss fine tuning, but for most of the world a service free at the point of need is an unimaginable pipe-dream. We speak of justice ('we should treat people rightly according to need') and equity ('we should provide equal access to healthcare according to need with financial factors being no deterrent'), but for most of the world such justice and equity are nothing more than a bad joke! For many, even if the resources are available in their country, the geographic barriers for rural people to reach those resources in the cities are insurmountable – and, more poignant still, so are the economic barriers. For many, the impossibility of access is akin to that of a shoeless lad from an urban slum standing outside a fancy downtown department store, gazing through the windows and ogling at the bright lights and fancy goods displayed within. He can look, but in terms of actual acquisition of these goods he might as well be a million miles away.

For others who launch on the path of expensive medical care, the situation may be likened to that of a country farmer who comes to town to seek out a relative or friend. He has only an address with no knowledge whatever of the layout of the city, so arriving at the bus station he boards a taxi, showing the driver the address. As the miles of crowded, confusing urban streets fly by, so the price on the taxi meter rises ever higher and far more rapidly than he could possibly have conceived. He has no means whatever of knowing whether the taxi driver is taking him by a direct route or simply driving him around the houses. Finally when he realizes his money is all spent, he has to alight at the roadside with empty pockets and no knowledge as to whether he is any nearer his destination than when he set out. Such situations provide a backcloth against which Christians can and do provide a loving concern for the disadvantaged and defenceless. The following story again illustrates this:

> The young man lived in the city with his married elder sister, both parents having died. In many countries when a girl marries, she traditionally severs all ties and responsibilities in her own family and becomes part and parcel of her husband's family, so having this younger brother living with them was a concession on the husband's part and one that could not be pushed too far. He worked in a tailor's shop but he began to develop recurrent bouts of abdominal pain. At the same time he began to lose weight and eventually his sister took him to a large hospital. Tuberculous peritonitis was diagnosed but all available finances were used in obtaining the diagnosis with nothing left for treatment.

Over a period of 18 months he continued to deteriorate without treatment. He could no longer work. He would lie awake at night groaning, and the husband was beginning to complain. At this point his sister brought him to one of our clinics. The sight of this emaciated figure who could hardly stand filled us with dismay. We had never had a patient like this before. His chance of survival looked small. One of the complications of the disease was intestinal obstruction – and almost certain death. In such a case surgery would be imperative but very difficult – and costly. Where could we refer him? We could think of nowhere. In cases of emergency for short term care we had various hospitals and doctor friends we could call on but nowhere was geared to the long term care of the chronic sick, at economic rates.

His sister looked at us imploringly. Would Jesus have refused? We capitulated. We loaded him into the LandRover and took him with us at the end of the day, groaning as he went.

The first few weeks were stormy. He couldn't eat anything except sips of tinned fruit juice. He had bouts of intense abdominal pain from which we doubted if he could recover, but again, through the grace of God and the patient persistence of staff members who refused to let him die, he slowly improved. Eventually he returned to his tailor's shop 15 kg heavier. In the light of pleading eyes, empty pockets and absence of alternative facilities we have found the Lord leading us on in trembling faith with very basic medical tools to cooperate with him and again and again, saying to us 'go and learn what this means, "I desire kindness".'[4]

For many nations the provision of healthcare comes low down the priority list for allocation of government resources. All too often defence necessarily ranks higher and the establishment of a firm industrial base that can provide the economic foundations for welfare services is a more urgent priority. This makes the problem of efficient use of available resources all the more important, and more often than not, the key issue in this is not so much one of economics and management as one of motivation and integrity.

There must be the motivation to provide a fair and good service – the best that is possible with the resources and available to as many as possible according to their need. The problem of remuneration of doctors and other medical workers is a vital one. If the doctor is paid according to item of service he is inclined to concentrate on those who can pay and on those services which are the most remunerative, neglecting other needs. If he is paid a stipend he lacks the motivation to serve and becomes a time-server rather than a people-server. This is where the Christian gospel has such a vital place in the development of effective worldwide healthcare services. By and large only true conversion to Christ will lead people into a lifetime of unselfish service on behalf of the disadvantaged and neglected. Only adequate spiritual nourishment will sustain such a life of service, yet without that motivation scarce resources are squandered, plundered and diverted into already well-supplied channels. This is where the ongoing international involvement of Christians is so vital; whether it be service in needy parts of the world for the sake of Christ, or the befriending of postgraduate students from countries with struggling economies, providing them with the spiritual resources to swim against the tide, and sustaining them by prayer and ongoing friendship. Economic issues are only really resolved with spiritual motivation.

Public health

It is not necessary here to reiterate in detail the enormous importance of the field of public health in the overall promotion of human health and welfare, or the outstanding successes that have been achieved down the years in the control of infectious disease, and in the elimination of basic causes of the spread of disease such as contaminated drinking water. The huge contribution of Christians and of medical missionaries worldwide in these areas is well documented in the relevant chapters of *Heralds of Health*.[5]

Public health is an area in any society in which the needs and rights of the individual have to be carefully balanced with the needs and rights of the community as a whole. Sometimes the two will be in open conflict and the appropriate balance will not necessarily be the same in all societies. A degree of coercion or curtailment of individual liberty that would be totally unacceptable in some communities may be justified where the risk to the viability of a society as a whole may be unacceptably high when the individual exercises his or her rights of personal choice.

It may be right, for example, in a Western society to allow parents the freedom to decline pertussis immunization for their child. It may not be appropriate in another situation to allow people the right to decline cholera vaccination in the face of an epidemic.

It may be common practice for the local river to be used for drinking water, cooking water, laundry and sewage disposal purposes indiscriminately. It may be more appropriate, however, for government health authorities committed to the welfare of the community to restrict the rights of the individual as to how he or she uses the river for the sake of the health of the whole community. It is the same principle employed by societies that use motorized transport in designating which side of the road you may drive on and which side you may not. This necessary curtailment of individual freedom of choice (more successful in some societies than others) is essential for the safety and welfare of all. The health authorities of many societies, however, face the temptation to exercise control with an unequal or unnecessarily heavy hand. We should be slow to judge the decisions of other societies, however, by the standards currently acceptable in our own. It is often necessary to understand the inner workings of a society and its needs before we can understand the rationale of apparently unjust or inequitable regulations.

Nowhere are the issues more clearly highlighted than in the area of population control. Most communities in the two-thirds world now recognize the need for population control as an essential for economic viability. This runs strongly counter, however, to the deeply ingrained assumptions of many traditional societies which see a large family as a mark of divine blessing and of future economic security. Measures have sometimes been Draconian, whether enforced or strongly pressured. These have included vasectomy in areas of rural India, or the strong advocation, verging on enforcement, of abortion for pregnant mothers already having a stated number of children. While compulsory abortion has never been official policy in China, there is little doubt that the rigidly applied one child family policy has led to intense social pressure for mothers to undergo abortion of subsequent pregnancies. It has also led to officially reported incidents of exposure of unwanted girl babies in the hope of having 'a son next time'. Nevertheless the one child family is seen as an essential to economic survival and the one child family generation is paying the price of the misguided population expansion policies of the previous generation. Who is to say where the line of curtailment of personal liberty and promotion of communal well-being is to be drawn? Ultimately it must be the people who live and work within particular communities who make those decisions, but it is the Christians *par excellence* who have the moral resources to make appropriate responses. They have the Bible, with its carefully interwoven themes of individual worth and community values. Christians have the Holy Spirit to guide them in their understanding of the Bible and to help them reach decisions of justice and equity relevant to their own situation.

Of enormous importance in this context is the contemporary Aids epidemic. Western medical circles debate endlessly the fine points of confidentiality in HIV testing and proscribe even the communication of information between involved professionals. Many struggling countries which the epidemic has barely reached would like to institute compulsory HIV testing as a necessary part of visa application, but are prevented from doing so by the weight of international opinion, the heavy amplification of Western voices, and the fear of very substantial economic loss were they to 'go it alone'. Is this not a situation where Western preoccupation with 'individual rights' is preventing international co-operation, and largely ignoring a public health time bomb until it is too late to do anything about it? While smallpox was still an international scourge a vaccination certificate was a universal requirement of international travel. Many Western countries require a clean X-ray for immigrants and sometimes visitors too. An HIV-negative certificate would not be foolproof, but might it not be an appropriate means of containment of this late twentieth-century scourge?

Smoking and alcohol

In the West, the ethics of punitive levels of taxation on tobacco and alcoholic products are frequently debated. Some propose them as a means of promoting public health. Governments are rarely willing to impose them to the extent of diminishing overall revenue, and therefore tend to settle for a policy of maximum returns that does very little to restrict consumption. Compulsory health warnings on cigarette advertisements and packets are a strange way of conveying two contradictory messages at the same time. In many countries there is no restriction of cigarette advertising on television and in not a few countries the marketing of tobacco products is a virtual government monopoly, and a very lucrative one. In many countries it would seem that almost the whole of the adult population, and many of the children too, smoke cigarettes.

The writer recalls watching a building site from the

balcony of a Chinese University student residents' block. One of the labourers had brought his four year old son along with him and left him at the side of the site to guard his jacket. While Dad was occupied the lad would feel in the jacket pockets, find the packet of cigarettes and matches and light up like a master of the art. Whenever Dad would look his way the cigarette would deftly disappear behind his back with an expression of innocence like that of many a Western teenager caught smoking behind the school gym. Yet this lad of only four was already so well practised in the art that his handling of the materials could have been that of an adult, and he was for sure no exception.

The public health challenges facing many such societies are overwhelming, and they call for Christian initiatives that will strike the right balance between the good of the individual and the welfare of all, and which are fired with a crusading spirit to change the world. In today's world most of such Christian initiative must come from within the community and Christians from outside can at best be catalysts who will show the pattern and will set the pace and allow local Christians to take the lead in changing their societies for good.

The environment

The statement at the outset of this book declares that 'we should respect God's creation for its own sake and for the benefit of our health'. This is one aspect of humanness and it follows that one aspect of health is the strength to respond appropriately to this imperative. Strength is needed primarily in two areas, economic and moral. Many traditional cultures regard the environment either as itself divine (that is, they are pantheists), or as controlled by spirit forces (that is, they are animists). The pantheist reveres nature and fears to initiate change for fear of offending the divinity. The animist seeks either to appease the spirit forces controlling natural events or to manipulate them. Both fall short of the Christian ideal of responsible stewardship of the environment under God who made it. For most societies in the two-thirds world, however, these traditional concepts are being swamped by a tide of materialism, either in the Marxist or capitalist framework, that regards the environment as inert or neutral, and therefore to be exploited or plundered at will for short-term economic gains. Such are the economic pressures on most of the world that it requires enormous moral courage to swim against the tide and to treat the environment responsibly, either in personal life or political decision-making. This moral calibre develops most readily in the framework of Christian convictions about God as Creator and our own role as stewards responsible to him for the care of the environment.

In a country where six million children are destitute vagabonds, the preservation of the rain forests does not rank so high on the political agenda. In a country where half the population is starving, and the import of adequate foodstuffs is economically impossible, the unwanted side effects of indiscriminate use of insecticides are usually ignored. In a country in the throes of an industrial revolution that is discovering the economic benefits of mass production and export, the effects of the pollution of air, soil and water are usually brushed aside in the euphoria created by employment, export and wage packets.

It is easy for those in the West to condemn the rape of the environment worldwide, but by and large the West lacks the moral courage to make it economically possible for the rest of the world to treat the planet with respect and gratitude. This is where Christians ought to be distinctively different, whether in a private capacity in supporting appropriate charities or in public life and influence of decision-making. Is our voice too little heard in this area? Are we more committed to our creature comforts than to our creator God? This is an area where moral courage will create economic possibilities, and where neglect will impinge heavily on the physical health of future generations.

Nursing

There is probably no profession on earth that epitomizes Christian ideals of loving practical service for fellow men and women as much as the profession of nursing. Where this is expressed in the context of predominantly non-Christian societies it stands out in striking contrast to prevailing attitudes and is a most powerful commendation of the truth and beauty of the gospel. Whatever ideals may be expressed, the dominant attitudes towards one's neighbour in non-Christian societies are either those of the government official or those of the market trader. The official sees his neighbour as one over whom to exercise power; the trader sees his neighbour as one from whom to extract money. The two are of course not totally mutually exclusive and both are easily carried over into professions where caring responsibility is recognized. The limits of that responsibility are clearly defined, most commonly in terms of close blood relationship. It is the Christian understanding of love for neighbour, expressed so vividly in the parable of the Good Samaritan, and worked out through centuries of Christian service, that has been the dominant motivating force in the spread of nursing services throughout the world. Where Christian hospitals have established lasting reputations in every corner of the globe, by and large it is to the nurses of those hospitals rather than to the doctors or other staff that individual patients turn in trust and gratitude. Christian nursing schools have been powerful forces in inculcating this approach in countless countries of the world, and not only in the context of medical care. Again and again the graduates of these schools have carried these values on into motherhood and passed them on to their own children. Where Christian influence has declined, nursing has tended to degenerate into a deskbound job, delegating every menial task to relatives of the patient rather than demonstrating how true nursing care can be applied.

The author recalls meeting at a conference in Singapore a Senior Nursing Administrator from Zambia and reminiscing on occasions twenty years earlier when he was a young doctor and she was a nursing student in Bulawayo. We reminisced of the lessons learned together then – lessons of going the second mile with patients, of running ward services, and of growing in faith through Bible study and fellowship. It was an enormous joy to see these lessons now being worked out at a senior level in Zambian nursing services.

Any review of current staffing needs overseas will immediately impress even the most sceptical reader that the day of missionary nurses is far from past. In every continent they are still needed, either for their direct nursing care or in a teaching role, and most often, and most effectively, where the one leads to the other.

The spectrum of medical services

We shall consider the subject matter of the two chapters on hospital medicine and primary care together, because within any society's structure of medical services, there is a spectrum. It ranges from very simple primary care up to tertiary care in centres of excellence, and it is not always possible to define where primary becomes secondary, and secondary becomes tertiary. In any society there is always a debate: not only on how much of total resources should be allotted to healthcare but, within that budget, how much should be put into primary services and how much into hospitals, teaching institutions, and centres of excellence. It is impossible to avoid hard decisions, and in countries where resources are extremely limited these decisions are harder still.

Before considering the priorities of the different aspects of a spectrum of medical care, it is worth asking what the relationship is between health and health services. This term 'health services' may be a misnomer, for it presupposes that the services provided are leading to improvements of health. The present author prefers the term 'medical services' because it more accurately describes what is being provided without pre-judging the issue as to whether in fact it is leading to improvements of health. That is of course the avowed overall aim. It may not be the aim of a considerable number of those who provide the services, however, and it is an aim that, in many circumstances, may be only very partially achieved.

In this book health is defined as 'the strength to be human', and humanness is defined in terms of relationships with God, with self, with others and with the environment. There are many circumstances in which 'health services' may provide the strength in terms of restored physical and mental function, but at the same time destroy the humanity in terms of relationships, thus negating the very purpose for which they were established. As the ladder is climbed from primary to tertiary medical services, the ability to restore physical and mental function may be increased, but the risks of losing or even destroying humanness in a maze of technical expertise are greatly increased too. Sensitive persons who work in large and high-tech institutions are acutely aware of these problems. The issues are similar throughout the world but as with so many other issues, where resources are scanty the potential for both good and evil is far greater.

For those involved in professional roles in the provision of medical care, it is difficult to grasp that, for most of the world, a level of primary care takes place long before medical professionals are approached. Indeed, in many parts of the world, providers of Western medicine, although they may have the stamp of government approval, are in fact the last resort when all else has failed.

Primary care begins in the home with Granny collecting herbs on the mountains or rubbing cow dung into the neonate's umbilicus. It is institutionalized in the village or regional herbalists, acupuncturists, shamans or witch doctors. It is deeply rooted in traditional cultures and closely tied to contemporary folk religion. Because both traditional cultures and folk religion have a lot to say about relationships they may do much to promote humanness. At the same time, however, they may neglect or undermine the strength to achieve that humanness. Granny's cow dung may produce neonatal tetanus. The shaman's raucous exorcism of headaches, caused by an intracranial tumour, will only exacerbate the aching head.

Most Western medical services in developing countries, whether Christian or government, have begun at the secondary level with hospital-based services. From earliest days many attempts have been made to break out of the hospital mould to reach out into the community both with preventive and educational programmes and with true primary care services. Only in the last thirty years, however, with the ever-mounting costs of surgical services and modern drugs have serious attempts been made to re-appraise the balance in division of resources. An excellent statement of this re-appraisal is found in the declaration of the consultation held in Wheaton, Illinois in 1981 and set out in full below:

1. Statement of values

Health is a state of physical, mental, emotional, and spiritual soundness. It is not merely the absence of disease or infirmity; neither is it dependent upon the absence of disability. We strongly affirm that Christians have the responsibility, based on the biblical revelation, the character of God, and the example and commands of Jesus Christ, to protect and promote health, especially for people who lack access to health care. To contribute meaningfully to the goal of providing healthcare in the next two decades for all the world's people it is necessary for Christian health ministries to rethink values, priorities, operational policies, and strategies. In proposing these new directions and opportunities for Christian health ministries in the developing world, we recognise that a similar situation also exists in developed countries. Substantial improvements in the health of people will require healthcare programmes that deal with a wide range of social, economic, and cultural, as well as medical problems. These programmes must be accessible to people in their home communities and be part of overall community development. Such programmes constitute community-based primary healthcare.

We identify ourselves with those who suffer from lack of such care. Christian healthcare ministries must work for the just allocation of health resources and services. We undertake to share information concerning the situations of the majority of the world's people with respect to their poverty, malnutrition, and premature death. We affirm the provision God has made in the natural world and through technology to eliminate these problems. We urge the adoption of the following practices in our healthcare ministries.

2. Patterns of primary health services

Community healthcare should include at least: education concerning prevailing health problems and the methods of identifying, preventing, and controlling them; promotion of food supply and proper nutrition; promotion of an adequate supply of safe water and basic sanitation; maternal and child healthcare, including family planning; immunisation against the major infectious diseases; prevention and control of locally endemic diseases; appropriate treatment of common diseases and injuries; and the provision of essential drugs.

Primary healthcare services require us to recognise individuals, families, churches, and communities as responsible partners. Wherever the church exists we see it as a vital catalyst for primary healthcare. In particular, the community and health workers in partnership will identify health problems, promote health measures, and identify trustworthy community based workers. The community must share responsibility for raising resources and maintaining and managing the activities and the workers.

Hospitals and other medical institutions form an important part of any health system. They are required for the care of difficult cases of illness referred to them by the community based health-care workers in the ordinary way. In addition, and where appropriate, hospital personnel may be involved in providing supervision, facilitating logistics, and organising training for the primary healthcare team.

The primary healthcare workers will be trained to teach preventive measures, to recognise common health problems, and to use appropriate curative measures including essential drugs. The primary healthcare programme should aim for coverage, effectiveness, and efficiency, and, above all, equity. Equity demands that input be directed most where the needs are greatest so that increasingly all people enjoy God's gift of health.

3. Roles of members of the health team

The concept of healthcare for all spreads the responsibility for health far beyond the confines of the traditional health professions. The burden of good health does not rest on health professionals alone. This means that believers with a wide variety of gifts, not only those with the gift of healing, have contributions to make to community healthcare. We envisage community healthcare maintained by mothers and others most concerned, supported by a variable team of local and external workers. These will be chosen for their spiritual and moral commitment to serve, trustworthy and compassionate character, and potential for learning, teaching, and service. The healthcare team might include:

a. Community health and development workers;

b. Pastors or others committed to spiritual ministries; and

c. People able to provide training and supervision in appropriate and necessary fields.

The healthcare team will work together with the community to promote concern and acceptance of responsibility for understanding the bases of health problems; to instruct in preventive and curative measures; to encourage or develop local skills; and to maintain Christlike patterns of caring.

4. Adaptation of healthcare programme to local conditions

We urge Christian health ministries to recognise the challenge of primary healthcare and in doing so to take the following actions:

a. Use every opportunity to strengthen primary healthcare programmes and ensure their integration into self-sustaining rural and urban developments.

b. Ensure that primary healthcare activities in which Christian health ministries are involved focus on problems of the highest priority as these are mutually perceived by the community, the local church, and the mission in cooperation with the national government. The activities of the healthcare programme should be culturally acceptable, technically appropriate, locally manageable, and implemented in such a way as to meet local needs.

c. Ensure that such activities are increasingly sustained by the community as their resources allow, thus fostering the principle of self-reliance. It is most important for the community to be involved in planning and implementing their own programme of healthcare. The mission should continue to function in a supportive role to the local church, responding to the needs of the community and encouraging a spirit of interdependence and cooperation.

5. Integration with government

As a consequence of the increasing commitment of governments to primary healthcare, new challenges and opportunities now exist for Christian health ministries. These ministries must seek to understand what governments are doing and to bring their policies into line with national healthcare policies. In doing so Christian health ministries will have many opportunities for service, including:

a. Opportunities to assist certain communities to develop appropriate programmes of community-based primary healthcare which may become models for adoption by similar communities elsewhere.

b. Opportunities to influence national policy toward truly wholistic care with equitable access to health by sharing their Christian distinctives and their own experience of working with local communities.

c. Opportunities to accept Christian responsibility within a national health programme for certain communities for specific purposes.

Conclusion

We recommend that all who are engaged in Christian health ministries review their priorities and the utilisation of their healthcare ministry resources, including both the human and financial resources, to promote and encourage primary healthcare programmes. This envisions current mission personnel themselves being encouraged to reorient their own healthcare priorities.[6]

A key statement at the end of Section 2 is 'the primary healthcare programme should aim for coverage, effectiveness, and efficiency, and, above all, equity. Equity demands that input be directed most where the needs are greatest'.

From a non-Christian framework, one of the most daring attempts to put this thinking into practice was Mao Tse-tung's launching of the barefoot doctor scheme in China. While not often literally barefooted, they were often almost barehanded and launched into the programme with not more than ten weeks of training. It is significant that in China today, while the scheme still exists and the training is being constantly upgraded, the reputation of the barefoot doctors among ordinary people is generally not high, and large numbers prefer to make often lengthy journeys to hospital outpatients. This may be a reflection of lack of confidence not only in the skills of these workers, but also their motivation. In this context it is interesting to note that in China today, in city after city, it is the former Christian hospitals that still carry the highest reputation. Although their formal Christian status was abolished more than forty years ago, the standards of personal care taught by the founders of these hospitals have stuck and been passed on to the present generation of staff. Those on the receiving end recognize this and are attracted to it.

The debate over the allocation of resources between primary care and hospital services will always be there and is a necessary part of seeking to establish equity in the provision of health services. The following extract from a Christian perspective in an area of limited resources gives some pointers on how to maximize resources in an equitable fashion:

1. Keep to essentials

Simplicity does not necessarily mean second-rate medicine. In our work of treating extra-pulmonary tuberculosis we used borrowed and only partly reliable X-ray and laboratory facilities. There was no operating theatre. We had one qualified nurse and one unqualified physiotherapist. However, in those inauspicious surroundings the results of treatment were comparable with those of any other centre in the world that had recorded its results. We sought to adapt our facilities and treatment to the realities of our patients' needs. We focused on disciplined clinical acumen, accurate history taking and careful examination supplemented with simple X-rays.

People wonder if medical missions are the end of the road professionally. Far from it. They are thrilling. Shorn of all the props and support and opportunities for referral, the clinician is thrown back on the basics of clinical diagnosis. He is forced to listen to and examine the patient carefully. On the basis of experience and with some reference to an often out-of-date textbook, he has to reach a diagnosis and decide on a plan of treatment within the scope of what is available. The reality of being a cooperator with God is often vivid. Simple structures can provide the framework in which the poor can come and not feel threatened. Simple structures work when the person who sits at the registry desk understands that this patient has had to come a three or four hour journey, and that if he can be seen within the next hour and a half he can get the last bus home that night and save himself a night at an inn and another day's work lost. This matters to the patient. When patients find that the staff – not just the doctors, but all the staff – are prepared to think of their situation to that extent they come back and they come back gratefully.

2. The provision of cheap accommodation for non-acute cases

I think of another institution that began life 80 years ago as a leprosarium. Some twenty years ago the institution developed a hospital providing care for leprosy patients on the one hand and post-polio rehabilitation and general orthopaedics on the other. The majority of staff were healed leprosy patients and dedicated Christians. Through careful husbanding of resources and willingness on the part of staff to go the second mile and work extremely hard the hospital was able to keep its costs down to one-fifth or one-tenth of those required at other medical facilities. Costs were further reduced by providing dormitory accommodation adjacent to the hospital for those requiring extensive physiotherapy or other non-acute treatment over an extended period. Not only was good treatment provided within the financial bracket of a large number of patients, but the message also came over loud and clear that Christians are ready to serve and to put the interests of others before their own interests.

3. Specialise in selected needy fields

The management of chronic conditions is generally an extremely needy area. Leprosy has long been a field in which Christian missions have made a major contribution. The need today is no less than before. Tuberculosis is an equally needy field. When we were led into the treatment of extra-pulmonary tuberculosis we found an immensely needy area that nobody else was touching and that could be dealt with using very simple tools. By focusing on one speciality, the contribution to the overall Christian testimony was multiplied manifold. This was not by virtue of any particular skills on our part; rather it was because people realised that we were seeking to meet the needs of a group of patients that nobody else could be bothered with. From time to time it brought newspaper reporters and television cameras and various other opportunities of testimony across the country.

I think too of a lady doctor who specialised in developing clinics for epilepsy patients. She gathered hundreds who had never before been treated, and enrolled them on regular medication. It led to control of the disease in large numbers of these hitherto untreated patients and became a testimony in government and medical circles up and down the country. Here was a Christian who cared and people noticed this. Other specialties worthy of particular attention are orthopaedics and ophthalmology. Where no other facilities exist a Christian hospital may have to provide a whole spectrum of medical and surgical treatment. This should not prevent the development of one or more of these specialties in the care of chronic disease. We cannot do everything but that is no excuse for doing nothing.

4. Involving the local church

In situations where a developed local church exists the relationship between that church and the Christian medical institution is an important one. Too easily the churches look on the mission institution as a means of cheap treatment for Christians, especially ordained ministers. Alternatively it may be seen as a source of income for Bible school or theological college. We need rather to challenge the churches to see the Christian medical institution as a channel for service to the community, an opportunity of expressing Christian concern for the needs of the unbelieving poor out in the heathen world. If the hospital is manifestly wealthier than the church it's not easy for the church to see any sense of responsibility towards the hospital. If the hospital is extending its arms to the needs of the poor to the extent that it itself is poverty stricken then the church is more likely to wake up to its responsibility. The sponsoring of charity beds is one possible line of development. Voluntary service in the hospital in an accessory capacity is another. In our case we had a regular rota of church ladies' groups coming to the hospital laundry. Others came at the annual bulk pickle-making time.

5. Spiritual support for doctors and their wives

The pressures on any doctor to conform to this world are tremendous. These pressures are many times greater in many developing situations. Again and again we-found a male doctor who would be prepared to give at least some part of his life to serve the poor in a rural hospital, but he could not go unless his wife was ready to go too or ready to see him go. In most cases the men and especially the women simply did not have the spiritual resources to resist the pressures of family, society and peers. We gave a great deal of time with our staff to Bible study, opening up the Gospels that they might see a pattern to follow. Again and again we found that the Word of God nourishes, challenges, strengthens and enables a trembling young Christian to resist those insidious attractions of money, fame and power. As we pray for medical missions I believe this should be one of our major prayer foci. Pray that moral calibre be built into the lives of young Christian doctors, nurses and medical personnel to stand against the tide of the world that swells around them, and enable them to leave all and follow Christ.[7]

217

It is this last section that is perhaps most important of all – the provision of spiritual resources for medical personnel to enable them to swim against the tide of materialism and to work not only for the correction of biochemical or biomechanical malfunction but also for their patients' spiritual well-being and integration as whole persons. This is a call then not only to provide people with the strength to be human but also to give them every encouragement to apply that strength to becoming integrated human beings in terms of the relationships suggested at the outset of this book – the fundamental relationships with God, with self, with others and with the environment. This is where Christians have distinct advantages; we know the way to forgiveness of sins and peace with God through the Lord Jesus Christ. We have learnt to accept ourselves in the knowledge that God has accepted us. We have tasted the nature of agape love and genuine truth which are the foundations of harmonious relationships with others, and we marvel at the environment in which we are placed and respect it as the creation of a holy and loving God. The roots of Western medicine are in the Christian concepts of truth and love. If these concepts are lost, Western medicine becomes a dangerous and even devilish tool in the hands of its practitioners. It is imperative that the hand of Christians involved in medical practice throughout the world is strengthened and their number and influence extended. They too need every assistance to become whole and integrated persons, living in the shalom of God, at harmony with themselves and one another and content with the surroundings in which they are placed. Only thus will they be qualified to be *health workers* as opposed to mere biomechanics and technicians tinkering with the machinery.

As we have seen so often in this chapter, people who live in areas where resources are plentiful are greatly advantaged. For many here access to Christian fellowship and Christian nurture is relatively easy. For those who are struggling in areas of poor resources, their problems may be compounded by a famine of the Word of God. This carries with it a dual imperative for Christians in advantaged situations. They need to take every opportunity to befriend medical workers from overseas who have come for postgraduate study, to love them, to be hospitable to them, to share with them the resources of their own rich spiritual heritage, and to pray for them when they return to their own country. Every Christian in the richer nations of the West needs also to examine his or her priorities and ask God if he or she should not be serving in some area of more limited resources. There not only can he or she seek to meet urgent physical needs but also can share his or her faith and attempt to equip followers of Christ within that community with spiritual resources to swim against the tide of selfish materialism. Thus people are helped not only to health – the strength to be human – but also to integrated humanity itself.

> *O strengthen me, that, while I stand*
> *Firm on the rock, and strong in Thee,*
> *I may stretch out a loving hand*
> *To wrestlers with the troubled sea.*
>
> *O use me, Lord, use even me,*
> *Just as thou wilt, and when, and where,*
> *Until thy blessèd face I see,*
> *Thy rest, thy joy, thy glory share.*

References

1 *Heralds of Health* (Christian Medical Fellowship, 1985) Foreword, pp. v–vi.
2 *Our Lord's, the Poor* (Christian Medical Fellowship, 1984), p. 7.
3 *Crisis Unawares* (OMF, 1981), pp. 86–88.
4 *Ibid.*, pp. 88–89.
5 *Heralds of Health* (Christian Medical Fellowship, 1985).
6 *New Directions and Opportunities for Christian Health Care Ministries* (MAP International, 1982), pp. 13–17.
7 *Our Lord's, the Poor* (Christian Medical Fellowship, 1984), pp. 9–11.

ABOUT THE CONTRIBUTORS

Andrew Fergusson, the editor of this volume, is General Secretary of the Christian Medical Fellowship. Before this he worked as a GP for nearly ten years in a Christian mission practice in South East London. He writes and broadcasts on a variety of medical ethics topics. His wife is a former anthropologist and they have two children in primary school.

David Atkinson is Fellow and Chaplain at Corpus Christ College, Oxford, a member of the Oxford Faculty of Theology, and a part-time lecturer in Pastoral Studies at Wycliffe Hall. He was for some years Theological Consultant to Care and Counsel, and helped to found the Oxford Christian Institute for Counselling. He is a member of the Society of Ordained Scientists, and author of a number of books, including *Pastoral Ethics in Practice*. He is married to Suzan, a teacher, lecturer and primary education consultant, and they have two grown-up children, Jonathan and Rachel.

Alan Storkey is a social scientist lecturing at Oak Hill College, where he co-ordinates Pastoral Studies. He helped to form the Movement for Christian Democracy, and is author of several books. Among his many interests he is an accomplished painter.

Michael Webb-Peploe, OBE, is a consultant physician and cardiologist. He is Physician in Charge, Cardiac Department, St Thomas's Hospital, London, and Honorary Civilian Consultant Cardiologist to the Army. His interests include hill walking, photography, and classical music.

Derek Munday is a General Practitioner in a large Christian practice in Reading. He is now the Honorary Executive Chairman of the multidisciplinary healthcare group, Christians in Caring Professions. His wife Mary is also a doctor.

Christine Chapman, CBE, OBE, has had over forty years experience in nursing in a variety of posts, the majority as a teacher of nurses. She served as a Council Member and Chairman of the Board of Education of the Royal College of Nursing (the last post for thirteen years). The final eighteen years were spent working in the Welsh National School of Medicine. This experience, along with membership of the General Medical Council and British Medical Association Medical Ethics Committee, has provided an insight into the world of the medical profession. A committed Christian since childhood she has worked in a voluntary capacity with Scripture Union and has been a member of the Nurses' Christian Fellowship since training days.

Huw Francis was educated at Fitzwilliam College, Cambridge University; Guy's Hospital Medical School, London; and the London School of Hygiene and Tropical Medicine. He held a number of posts in English public health, including senior lecturer in community medicine, Manchester University and Area Medical Officer of the former Camden and Islington Area Health Authority (Teaching). He served on a number of Government committees. On the re-organization of the NHS in 1982, he returned to clinical medicine, mainly in occupational health. He has published papers on preventive medicine, medical ethics and the history of public health.

R. J. Berry is Professor of Genetics, University College, London, and formerly Professor at the Royal Free Hospital School of Medicine, University of London. From 1990 to 1992 he was President of the European Ecological Federation, and currently is a member of the Human Fertilization and Embryology Authority. His recent books include *Real Science, Real Faith* (Monarch, 1991) and *Environmental Dilemmas* (Chapman & Hall, 1992).

Peter Pattisson qualified in medicine at Cambridge in the early 1960s and worked for Save The Children Fund in Korea. He was awarded the OBE in 1977, and now works as a GP in Pembury, Kent, retaining a strong interest in the healthcare scene worldwide.